S0-BOZ-868

WITHDRAWN

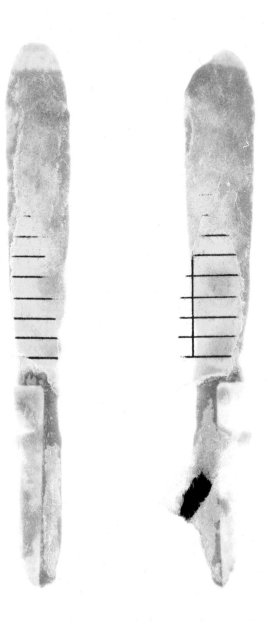

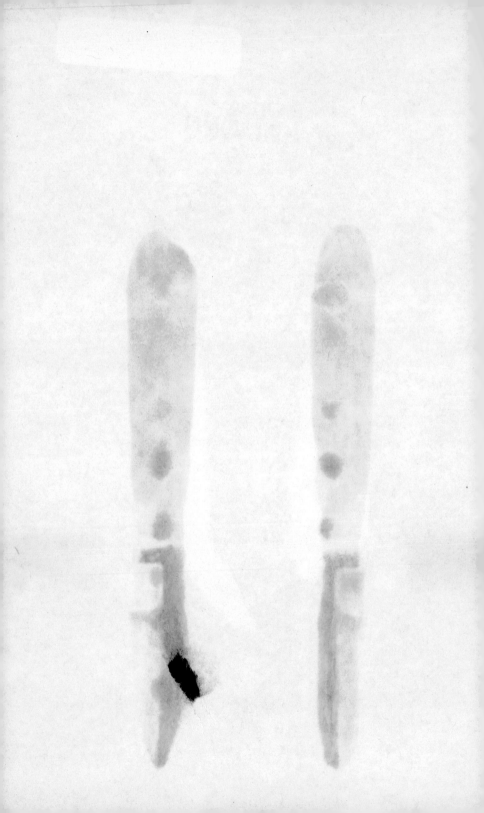

THE ROSSETTI-MACMILLAN LETTERS

THE ROSSETTI-MACMILLAN LETTERS

<><>

*Some 133 Unpublished Letters Written to
Alexander Macmillan, F. S. Ellis, and Others,
by Dante Gabriel, Christina, and William
Michael Rossetti, 1861–1889*

<><>

EDITED, WITH AN INTRODUCTION AND NOTES
by Lona Mosk Packer

UNIVERSITY OF CALIFORNIA PRESS
BERKELEY AND LOS ANGELES 1963

To James E. Packer

❖❖❖

University of California Press
Berkeley and Los Angeles, California

Cambridge University Press, London, England

© *1963 by The Regents of the University of California*

Library of Congress Catalog Card No. 63-21222

Printed in the United States of America

PREFACE

⋄◈⋄

When I was in London during 1958–60 gathering material for a biography of Christina Rossetti, I wrote to Macmillan & Co., inquiring whether the London firm had any correspondence from her, and was told there was a packet of letters in the files. The firm kindly gave me permission to examine, copy, and reproduce the material for publication. Much to my surprise, I found one hundred and twenty letters from Christina, William Michael, and Dante Gabriel Rossetti. Unpublished and unread, they had been preserved in the Macmillan archives for almost a century, unknown even to the present proprietors of the firm. Although I have drawn upon the correspondence in writing my biography and have published brief excerpts from it in articles, as a group the letters remain unpublished.

The correspondence covers the years from 1861 to 1889. Because with one exception, Macmillan published all Christina's volumes of poetry, by far the greater number of letters are written by her, sixty-eight, to be exact. William Michael, who published two books with Macmillan, is the author of twenty-five letters. The remaining twenty-seven are written by Dante Gabriel Rossetti. Although Macmillan was not his publisher and therefore his letters in the present collection do not refer to publication of his own work, as the illustrator of Christina's volumes he had occasion to correspond with the publisher frequently, particularly during the 1860's. Of special interest to students of literature are his 1864 letters urging Macmillan to publish the young and then unknown Swinburne and an earlier group of letters dealing with the publication and reviews of Gilchrist's *Blake,* to which the Rossetti brothers contributed.

Although many of Dante Gabriel's letters treat in somewhat technical terms of design and other matters relating to book production, they are nonetheless written in the bold, dashing, vigorous, and colloquial style characteristic of his personal correspondence; and they provide additional knowledge of his complex personality. We see him in these letters neither as the painter of romantic subjects nor as the poet of esoteric sonnets, but as a skilled craftsman discussing the technical details of his craft.

Christina's letters likewise reveal an unfamiliar aspect of her enigmatic personality. She appears in them as the working poet with a business-like interest in preparing her books for publication. Her lively concern with revising her poems and with retaining copyright—her "hobby" she called it—discloses the strain of practicality she shared with her brothers. At the same time her letters possess her own unique flavor, a combination of courteous deference, playfulness, subtle insight, and feminine wit. Although William's letters bear to a less marked degree the imprint of his individuality, they too display unexplored facets of his personality. Through them we come to appreciate a blunt independence, a sharp decisiveness, and a dry good-humor not always discernible in his numerous published works.

The tone of these letters expresses not only the individual personalities of the writers but also their differing attitudes toward publishers and publishing. Christina's attitude of grateful respect contrasts amusingly with Dante Gabriel's assured condescension, slightly tinged with hauteur, and with William's brusque efficiency.

Unfortunately Macmillan's share in the correspondence is not extant, chiefly because the Rossettis had a habit of destroying their letters. However, I have included in this edition a few letters from Macmillan's privately published correspondence which shed light upon the relationship. I have likewise inserted a group of fifteen letters from Christina to F. S. Ellis, fourteen of them written at the time she left Macmillan for Ellis. This correspondence fills in what would otherwise appear as an inexplicable gap in the sequence. Some additional letters reprinted in whole or in part from various sources, both published and unpublished, have the same function, that of supplementing and clarifying the series.

The arrangement is chronological. I have been obliged to supply conjectural dates for a number of undated or partially dated letters. In many instances I was guided by memoranda or marginal notes written on the letters by either Macmillan or a member of his firm, in others by the postmark on the envelope. Failing this information, I relied upon internal evidence, and when this was not available either upon the probable place of the letter in the context of the series or upon my general knowledge of its relation to established facts and events. Only when the date is clearly open to doubt, have I felt called upon to provide a fully detailed explanation for conjectural dating.

My editorial practice has been to reproduce the original as it appears in manuscript, following meticulously the letter headings and peculiarities of spelling and punctuation, exactly as written. I have included most of the deleted passages, excluding only the obviously insignificant and the false starts. Often the crossed-out passages are relevant or psychologically illuminating, and in general they give the reader a more intimate glimpse of the writer's mind at work than he could otherwise obtain. (Crossed-out words or passages are enclosed within pointed brackets so: <wrote>.) Acting upon the assumption that the reader prefers not to have his attention distracted by editorial comment, as a general rule I have not emphasized deviations by inserting *sic* in the text except in cases which would otherwise puzzle the reader. Square brackets enclose conjectural dates and extraneous matter whenever it is included in the text.

Both the writer of the letter and the person addressed are

stated, following the number. In all instances, except when the letter belongs to the Macmillan archives, the source of the text is given. When the source does not appear, it may be understood that the letter belongs to the Macmillan collection.

I wish to acknowledge here my gratitude to Macmillan & Co., Ltd. for permission to publish the letters and to Lovat Dickson and Timothy Farmiloe for special assistance in making them available to me. I also wish to thank the firm for permission to use extracts from Alexander Macmillan's privately published correspondence, and to thank the proprietors and editors of the *Times Literary Supplement, PMLA, Notes and Queries, Victorian Studies, The Western Humanities Review,* and *Collier's Encyclopedia* for permitting me to reprint material which originally appeared in their publications. I am obliged to Janet Camp Troxell and the Harvard University Press and to Cecil Y. Lang and the Yale University Press for allowing me to reprint correspondence from the *Three Rossettis* and *The Swinburne Letters.*

I am grateful to the Rossetti family for making available to me the documents and family papers in their possession and to the three Rossettis' literary executors, Helen Rossetti Angeli and Harold Rossetti, for copyright permission. I owe thanks to Evelyn Courtney-Boyd of Penkill Castle, Ayrshire, for permission to publish two letters from F. S. Ellis to Alice Boyd and to examine the manuscripts in the Penkill Library. For critical help and suggestions, information, or general assistance I am obliged to Jack Adamson, Andrée Barnett, Gill Bridge, Helen Fetherstanhaugh, Harold Folland, Earl Leslie Griggs, Robert Helbling, Virginia Jacobsen, Milton Voigt, Donald Walker, and particularly to William E. Fredeman for knowledge freely shared and for patient skill in detecting and correcting inaccuracies before their interment in print. I wish also to thank Sally Allen and Helen Winn for typing assistance done with a critical eye.

I would like to express appreciation to M. L. Hoyle and the staff of the Students' Room of the British Museum for placing at my disposal the unpublished correspondence of the Ashley

Library and for other courtesies; to R. W. Hunt, Keeper of Western Manuscripts, and his staff at the Bodleian Library, Oxford, to Ann Bowden and staff at the Humanities Research Center, University of Texas, to Elizabeth Fry and the librarians of the Manuscript Room at the Huntington Library, San Marino, California, to the Boston Public Library, the staff of the Bancroft Library, University of California, Berkeley, and to the late L. H. Kirkpatrick and staff at the University of Utah, particularly Alva C. Dean and assistants, Harold Bell, Virginia Boyd, and Merle Earnshaw.

I am grateful to the Committee on the Use of Literary Manuscripts, University of Texas, for permitting me to reproduce material belonging to the Humanities Research Center, and to Professor C. A. Cline for assistance in examining the collection there.

Finally I am happy to acknowledge the financial assistance given me through three research grants from the American Philosophical Society, and further grants from the American Council of Learned Societies and the University of Utah Research Committee.

L. M. P.

Salt Lake City
October, 1962

CONTENTS

List of Letters .... *xiii*

Abbreviations .... *xix*

Introduction *1*

THE LETTERS

    1861–1864 12

    1865 36

    1866–1869 57

    1870–1871 72

    1874–1876 97

    1876–1881 119

    1882–1889 142

Index *159*

LIST OF LETTERS

	Date	Author	Recipient	Page
1.	[December, 1861]	Christina Rossetti	Alexander Macmillan	13
2.	July 2, 1863	Christina Rossetti	Alexander Macmillan	14
3.	August 7 [1863]	W. M. Rossetti	Alexander Macmillan	15
4.	October 14, 1863	D. G. Rossetti	Alexander Macmillan	16
5.	October 29 [1863]	W. M. Rossetti	Alexander Macmillan	17
6.	December 1 [1863]	Christina Rossetti	Alexander Macmillan	19
6A.	December 1, 1863	Christina Rossetti	Alexander Macmillan	20
7.	January 21 [1864]	W. M. Rossetti	Alexander Macmillan	21
8.	March [1864]	D. G. Rossetti	Alexander Macmillan	21
9.	April 4 [1864]	Christina Rossetti	Alexander Macmillan	22
10.	[April] 8 [1864]	Christina Rossetti	Alexander Macmillan	23
11.	[June, 1864]	Christina Rossetti	Alexander Macmillan	23
12.	Wednesday [1864]	Christina Rossetti	Alexander Macmillan	24
13.	Wednesday [1864]	D. G. Rossetti	Alexander Macmillan	25
14.	June 3, 1864	Alexander Macmillan	D. G. Rossetti	25
15.	June 29, 1864	D. G. Rossetti	Alexander Macmillan	26
16.	[Summer, 1864]	D. G. Rossetti	Alexander Macmillan	16
17.	July 13 [1864]	D. G. Rossetti	Alexander Macmillan	27
18.	August 24, 1864	D. G. Rossetti	Alexander Macmillan	28
19.	September 5, 1864	D. G. Rossetti	Alexander Macmillan	29
20.	September 7, 1864	D. G. Rossetti	Alexander Macmillan	29
21.	[September, 1864]	D. G. Rossetti	Alexander Macmillan	30
22.	September 9 [1864]	W. M. Rossetti	Alexander Macmillan	30
23.	September 15, 1864	D. G. Rossetti	A. C. Swinburne	31
24.	November 17 [1864]	Christina Rossetti	Alexander Macmillan	31
25.	November 29 [1864]	W. M. Rossetti	Alexander Macmillan	32
26.	Wednesday [December, 1864]	Christina Rossetti	Alexander Macmillan	33
27.	[December] 20 [1864]	Christina Rossetti	Alexander Macmillan	34

	Date	Author	Recipient	Page
28.	Monday [December, 1864]	Christina Rossetti	Alexander Macmillan	35
29.	[January] 7, 1865	Christina Rossetti	Alexander Macmillan	37
30.	January 11, 1865	D. G. Rossetti	Alexander Macmillan	38
31.	[January] 14 [1865]	Christina Rossetti	Alexander Macmillan	39
32.	January 24, 1865	D. G. Rossetti	Alexander Macmillan	40
33.	February 3, 1865	D. G. Rossetti	Alexander Macmillan	40
34.	February 11, 1865	D. G. Rossetti	Alexander Macmillan	42
35.	February 26, 1865	D. G. Rossetti	Alexander Macmillan	43
36.	February 26 [1865]	W. M. Rossetti	Alexander Macmillan	43
37.	Tuesday morning [March, 1865]	Christina Rossetti	Alexander Macmillan	44
38.	[March] 23 [1865]	Christina Rossetti	Alexander Macmillan	45
39.	March 27 [1865]	D. G. Rossetti	Alexander Macmillan	46
40.	Monday [March, 1865]	Christina Rossetti	Alexander Macmillan	47
41.	[March] 30 [1865]	Christina Rossetti	Alexander Macmillan	47
42.	March 31, 1865	D. G. Rossetti	Alexander Macmillan	48
43.	April 4, 1865	D. G. Rossetti	Alexander Macmillan	49
44.	April 26, 1865	D. G. Rossetti	Alexander Macmillan	50
45.	April 28, 1865	D. G. Rossetti	Alexander Macmillan	50
46.	Wednesday night [April–May, 1865]	Christina Rossetti	D. G. Rossetti	51
47.	April 30 [1865]	W. M. Rossetti	Alexander Macmillan	52
48.	July 10 [1865]	W. M. Rossetti	Alexander Macmillan	53
49.	December 3, 1865	D. G. Rossetti	Alexander Macmillan	54
50.	December 5, 1865	Christina Rossetti	Alexander Macmillan	55
51.	December 16 [1865]	Christina Rossetti	Alexander Macmillan	56
52.	January 3, 1866	Christina Rossetti	Alexander Macmillan	58
53.	January 3, 1866	Christina Rossetti	[Thomas Niles]	58
54.	January 19 [1866]	Christina Rossetti	David Masson	60
55.	Tuesday January 30, 1866	D. G. Rossetti	Alexander Macmillan	61
56.	March 29, 1866	D. G. Rossetti	Alexander Macmillan	61
57.	April 5, 1866	D. G. Rossetti	Alexander Macmillan	62
58.	April 21 [1866]	D. G. Rossetti	Alexander Macmillan	62
59.	July 24, 1866	D. G. Rossetti	Alexander Macmillan	63
60.	Friday morning [December, 1866]	Christina Rossetti	Alexander Macmillan	64
61.	June 7 [1867]	W. M. Rossetti	Alexander Macmillan	65
62.	June 10 [1867]	W. M. Rossetti	Alexander Macmillan	65
62A.	June 10 [1867]	W. M. Rossetti	Alexander Macmillan	66
63.	June 11 [1867]	W. M. Rossetti	Alexander Macmillan	67
64.	Saturday evening [July 1, 1867]	Christina Rossetti	The Firm	69
65.	[Spring, 1868]	Christina Rossetti	Alexander Macmillan	69
66.	Thursday morning [Autumn, 1868]	Christina Rossetti	Alexander Macmillan	70
67.	September 5, 1869	W. M. Rossetti	Alexander Macmillan	70

Date	Author	Recipient	Page
68. February 23, 1870	Christina Rossetti	F. S. Ellis	74
69. February 25, 1870	Christina Rossetti	F. S. Ellis	75
70. Monday evening February 28, 1870	Christina Rossetti	F. S. Ellis	76
71. March 3, 1870	Christina Rossetti	F. S. Ellis	76
72. March 7, 1870	Christina Rossetti	F. S. Ellis	77
73. Monday morning [Spring, 1870]	Christina Rossetti	D. G. Rossetti	79
74. Saturday evening [March, 1870]	Christina Rossetti	F. S. Ellis	79
75. Wednesday [March 23, 1870]	D. G. Rossetti	Christina Rossetti	81
76. March 29, 1870	Christina Rossetti	F. S. Ellis	81
77. March 29, 1870	Christina Rossetti	Alexander Macmillan	83
78. Wednesday evening [April, 1870]	Christina Rossetti	F. S. Ellis	84
79. Friday [April] 29 [1870]	Christina Rossetti	F. S. Ellis	85
80. Saturday night [April 30, 1870]	Christina Rossetti	F. S. Ellis	85
81. Saturday night [May, 1870]	Christina Rossetti	F. S. Ellis	81
82. May 14, 1870	F. S. Ellis	Alice Boyd	86
83. May 25, 1870	F. S. Ellis	Alice Boyd	87
84. June 1, 1870	Christina Rossetti	F. S. Ellis	88
85. Wednesday morning [Summer, 1870]	Christina Rossetti	F. S. Ellis	90
86. December 30, 1870	D. G. Rossetti	Alexander Macmillan	91
87. March 2, 1871	Christina Rossetti	F. S. Ellis	92
88. April 26, 1871	Christina Rossetti	[Dalziel Brothers]	93
89. August 3, 1871	Christina Rossetti	[Dalziel Brothers]	94
90. November 5 [1871]	W. M. Rossetti	Alexander Macmillan	95
91. December 1, 1871	Christina Rossetti	Alexander Macmillan	96
92. February 3, 1874	Christina Rossetti	Alexander Macmillan	98
93. February 4, 1874	Christina Rossetti	Alexander Macmillan	99
94. April 20, 1874	Christina Rossetti	Alexander Macmillan	100
95. Monday, July 27 [1874]	Christina Rossetti	Alexander Macmillan	101
96. October 29, 1874	W. M. Rossetti	Alexander Macmillan	102
97. Friday evening [Autumn, 1874]	Christina Rossetti	Alexander Macmillan	103
98. Friday, January 22, 1875	Christina Rossetti	Alexander Macmillan	104
99. January 26, 1875	Christina Rossetti	Alexander Macmillan	105
100. January 30, 1875	Christina Rossetti	Alexander Macmillan	107
101. March 25, 1875	Christina Rossetti	Alexander Macmillan	108
102. May 22, 1875	W. M. Rossetti	George Grove	109
103. June 3, 1875	W. M. Rossetti	George Grove	110

	Date	Author	Recipient	Page
104.	June 10, 1875	Christina Rossetti	[? Routledge Brothers]	111
105.	Tuesday 16 [1875]	Christina Rossetti	Alexander Macmillan	112
106.	Tuesday 24 [1875]	Christina Rossetti	Alexander Macmillan	112
107.	August 27 [1875]	Christina Rossetti	Alexander Macmillan	113
108.	Saturday morning [1875]	Christina Rossetti	Alexander Macmillan	114
109.	Tuesday morning [1875]	Christina Rossetti	Alexander Macmillan	115
110.	September 12, 1875	W. M. Rossetti	George Grove	116
111.	November 29, 1875	Alexander Macmillan	Ellice Hopkins	116
112.	Saturday evening [1875]	Christina Rossetti	Alexander Macmillan	117
113.	Tuesday [December] 7 [1875]	Christina Rossetti	Alexander Macmillan	118
114.	November 4, 1876	Christina Rossetti	Alexander Macmillan	120
115.	July 6 [After 1876]	Christina Rossetti	[?]	122
116.	December 12, 1877	Christina Rossetti	Alexander Macmillan	122
117.	Wednesday [December, 1877]	Christina Rossetti	Alexander Macmillan	123
118.	April 26, 1878	Christina Rossetti	Alexander Macmillan	123
119.	January 16, 1879	W. M. Rossetti	The Firm	124
120.	January 24 [1879]	W. M. Rossetti	Alexander Macmillan	125
121.	Saturday August 23 [1879]	Christina Rossetti	The Firm	125
122.	December 17, 1879	Christina Rossetti	D. G. Rossetti	126
123.	December 26, 1879	Christina Rossetti	D. G. Rossetti	127
124.	September 10, 1880	W. M. Rossetti	George Grove	128
125.	September 20, 1880	W. M. Rossetti	George Grove	129
126.	November, 1880	W. M. Rossetti	The Editor	131
127.	November, 1880	Harry Quilter	The Editor	132
128.	April 18, 1881	Christina Rossetti	Alexander Macmillan	133
129.	April 20, 1881	Christina Rossetti	Alexander Macmillan	133
130.	Saturday, April 23, 1881	Christina Rossetti	Alexander Macmillan	135
131.	April 26, 1881	Christina Rossetti	Alexander Macmillan	136
132.	April 27, 1881	Christina Rossetti	Alexander Macmillan	137
133.	Saturday [1881]	Christina Rossetti	Alexander Macmillan	137
134.	June 17, 1881	Christina Rossetti	[Charles Fairfax Murray]	138
135.	July 22 [1881]	Christina Rossetti	George Lillie Craik	139
136.	August 17, 1881	Christina Rossetti	Alexander Macmillan	140
137.	June 3, 1882	W. M. Rossetti	George Lillie Craik	143
138.	July 27, 1882	Christina Rossetti	Alexander Macmillan	144
139.	July 29, 1882	Christina Rossetti	Alexander Macmillan	144
140.	Monday, September 18 [1882]	Christina Rossetti	[? George Grove]	145
141.	October 11, 1882	Christina Rossetti	[? George Grove]	146
142.	October 11, 1882	Christina Rossetti	Ella Farman Pratt	147
143.	November 3, 1882	Christina Rossetti	[? George Grove]	148

	Date	Author	Recipient	Page
144.	January 16, 1883	Christina Rossetti	Alexander Macmillan	148
145.	January 22, 1883	Christina Rossetti	F. S. Ellis	149
146.	December 15, 1884	W. M. Rossetti	Alexander Macmillan	151
147.	[January, 1885]	Christina Rossetti	Alexander Macmillan	152
148.	October 14, 1886	Christina Rossetti	The Firm	152
149.	Tuesday, [? 1886/1888]	Christina Rossetti	William Bryant	153
150.	November 24 [1886]	Christina Rossetti	The Firm	154
151.	August 16 [1887]	Christina Rossetti	Alexander Macmillan	155
152.	Monday morning [August, 1887]	Christina Rossetti	Alexander Macmillan	155
153.	December 19, 1888	Christina Rossetti	Alexander Macmillan	156
154.	May 24, 1889	W. M. Rossetti	Alexander Macmillan	158

ABBREVIATIONS

Note.—Unless otherwise stated, the place of publication is London.

Add. MS	Additional manuscript, British Museum.
AM	Alexander Macmillan.
Ash. MSS	The Ashley Library collection, British Museum Dept. of MSS, T. J. Wise Catalogue, 9 vols. (1922–1927).
Ath.	*The Athenæum.*
Bell	Mackenzie Bell, *Christina Georgina Rossetti* (1898).
Bod. MSS	Bodleian Library manuscripts, Oxford.
Bod. Ross. MSS	Rossetti documents on loan to the Bodleian; owned by Mrs. Helen Rossetti Angeli.
Brit. Mus. MSS	British Museum manuscripts.
CGR	Christina Georgina Rossetti.
DGR	Dante Gabriel Rossetti.
DGRFL	*Dante Gabriel Rossetti's Family Letters with a Memoir,* ed. W. M. Rossetti, 2 vols. (1895).
Doughty, *Lttrs. to Ellis*	Oswald Doughty, *The Letters of D. G. Rossetti to His Publisher, F. S. Ellis* (1928).

Fam. Lttrs.	*The Family Letters of Christina Georgina Rossetti,* ed. W. M. Rossetti (1908).
GM	Christina Rossetti, *Goblin Market* (1862).
Graves	C. L. Graves, *The Life and Letters of Alexander Macmillan* (1910).
Lang	*The Swinburne Letters,* ed. Cecil L. Lang, 6 vols. (New Haven, Yale University Press, 1959–1962).
Lttrs. to Allnghm.	*Dante Gabriel Rossetti's Letters to William Allingham,* ed. George Birbeck Hill (1897).
Macm. Cat.	James Foster, *A Bibliographical Catalogue of Macmillan & Company's Publications from 1843 to 1880* (1891).
Macm. Lttrs., Glasgow ed.	*Letters of Alexander Macmillan,* ed. George Macmillan (Glasgow, privately printed, 1908).
Morgan	Charles Morgan, *The House of Macmillan, 1843–1943* (New York, 1944).
N&Q	*Notes and Queries.*
Christina Rossetti	Lona Mosk Packer, *Christina Rossetti* (Berkeley and Los Angeles, University of California Press, 1963). All references by short title are to this work.
Penn. Hist. Soc.	The Pennsylvania Historical Society.
Penk. Lib. MSS	The Penkill Library manuscripts, owned by Miss Evelyn Courtney-Boyd of Penkill Castle, Ayrshire.
PMLA	Publications of the Modern Language Association of America.

PR PR	Christina Rossetti, *Prince's Progress* (1866).
Ross. Pprs.	*The Rossetti Papers, 1862–1870,* ed. W. M. Rossetti (1903).
Remin.	W. M. Rossetti, *Some Reminiscences,* 2 vols. (1906).
SP LK	Christina Rossetti, *Speaking Likenesses* (1874).
TLS	*The Times Literary Supplement.*
Troxell	Janet Camp Troxell, *Three Rossettis* (Cambridge, Harvard University Press, 1937).
Univ. Texas MSS	Manuscripts at the Humanities Research Center, owned by the University of Texas.
WHR	*Western Humanities Review.*
WMR	William Michael Rossetti.
Works	Christina Georgina Rossetti, *The Poetical Works,* ed. W. M. Rossetti (1904).

INTRODUCTION

❖❖❖

William Michael was the first Rossetti to meet Alexander Macmillan in 1854. William, then twenty-five, was spending a few days at Cambridge with his friend John Ferguson McClennan, who moved in a circle of brilliant young University men. He introduced William to the more noted among them and also to Alexander Macmillan, then "a rising young publisher in the town," whose house at Number One Trinity-Street, combination of bookshop and publishers' quarters, had already become a genial gathering place for Cambridge wits, many of whom, as Charles Morgan says, came into the bookseller's shop to buy books and remained with the publishing house to write them.

Up to that time Alexander had regarded himself as the less gifted brother of Daniel, that "grave black man," whose stubbornly spectacular battle with poverty and ill-health eventually gained for the Macmillan brothers their precarious position of debt-ridden independence as reputable Cambridge booksellers and publishers. Although Daniel, friend of Maurice and Kingsley and advocate of "muscular Christianity," considered poverty wholesome for the soul, Alexander took a more practical view of the matter. Larger rooms, better clothing, and better food may not constitute happiness, he told his brother, "but after all, tight circumstances, no more than tight boots are comfortable"; and in 1854 with *Westward*

1

Ho! in the press, he looked forward with anticipatory pleasure to more "tolerably easy circumstances."

Of sturdy, pious Scottish peasant stock, both boys were familiar early in life with the bitter bite of poverty. Starting as a poorly paid schoolmaster at sixteen, Alexander was subsequently a chemist's assistant, a sailor, and an usher at a small school. After a disheartening trip to America as a deckhand, he found himself at eighteen roaming the streets of Glasgow, penniless, looking for any kind of work and willing to take a porter's job at six shillings a week. At twenty he was hopelessly drudging away as a schoolmaster in a poverty-ridden collier's district in Nitshill. Meanwhile Daniel, who had gone to London to seek his fortune, not only obtained for himself a modest foothold at Seeley's bookselling shop on Fleet Street, but also succeeded in getting Alexander taken on as a clerk at sixty pounds a year. And so the young schoolmaster left for London, little dreaming that one day his grand-nephew would be directing the destiny of the nation from No. 10 Downing Street.

But the brothers' struggles were just beginning. They started in 1843 with a small bookshop in Aldersgate Street. That same year, borrowing heavily, they bought out Mr. Newby's business at Number Seventeen Trinity-Street, Cambridge, and published their first book. Taking in a partner in 1845, they purchased Mr. Stevenson's business at Number One Trinity-Street. By 1854 Daniel's health had declined to the point at which he was unable to direct the affairs of the business. By 1855 he was fighting for his life. Two years later he died, and Alexander, who had increasingly shouldered the heavy responsibilities of the expanding business, became the head of the firm. Freed from the loving domination of his elder brother's powerful, puritanical personality, Alexander developed rapidly into what the historian J. E. Green called "the pet publisher of the day at Cambridge."

At the time William Michael first met Macmillan, the Rossetti family was also struggling to escape the strangle hold of poverty. In straitened circumstances since 1846, when owing

2

to failing health and incipient blindness, the father Gabriele Rossetti, noted Italian poet-patriot and Dante commentator, had lost his position as professor of Italian at King's College, the Rossettis, no less than the Macmillans, had felt the tight pinch of the boot. But with Gabriele's death in 1854, the family's prospects brightened. His widow, Frances Lavinia, inherited a small estate from her parents, both of whom died that same year; William was promoted at the Excise Office where he had been a government clerk since his fifteenth year; and the Rossettis too could look forward to enjoying "more tolerably easy circumstances."

Of the four children, Maria, the eldest, had been supporting herself as a governess for almost a decade. In addition to carrying out his duties at the Excise Office, William, youthful ex-editor of the defunct *Germ* (1850), was gaining a reputation as a knowledgeable art reviewer, first on *The Critic* and then on *The Spectator*. By 1854 the twenty-six-year-old Dante Gabriel, already known as a painter of distinction, and the twenty-four-year-old Christina, a poet since she was twelve, had already written some of their best poetry. But except for poems in the experimental *Germ*, one of the most successful failures in English literary history, the work of neither poet was widely published. Christina had placed a few poems with *The Athenæum*, and in 1847 her grandfather, Gaetano Polidori, had published a privately printed volume of her youthful poetry for family circulation. After the collapse of *The Germ*, some of Gabriel's early masterpieces appeared in the second Pre-Raphaelite organ, the 1856 *Oxford and Cambridge Magazine*, but the greater part of his poetry remained unpublished until 1870, destined to eight years of darkness in his wife's tomb, where he was to bury it at her death in 1862.

After William's Cambridge visit in 1854, we hear little about the Rossetti-Macmillan acquaintance until 1861. In the intervening years Alexander had started *Macmillan's Magazine*, with David Masson as first editor, and had opened his branch office in London at 23 Henrietta Street, Covent Garden, where he soon began to hold his famous Thursday evening "Tobacco Parliaments." Taking a weekly trip to London, on Thursdays he was "at home to all and sundry"; and providing the foremost poets, scientists, artists, novelists, and scholars of the day with "tea and stronger fluids, with occasional tobacco," he encouraged discussions of "Darwin and conundrums with general jollity intermixed." As at Cambridge, so in London he created a genial, intellectually exciting center for a circle of productive men.

Gabriel's artist friends, Thomas Woolner, Holman Hunt, and Alexander Munro, all attended these "Tobacco Parliaments" with some regularity, and he accompanied them from time to time. It was probably at one of the Henrietta Street Thursday evening gatherings that Gabriel discussed with Macmillan the possible publication of his *Early Italian Poets* (reissued in 1874 as *Dante and His Circle*). Already in 1854 the publisher had expressed interest in the forthcoming translation, and in 1861 Gabriel offered it to him. "My first offer of it will be to Macmillan, with whom I have had some talk," he confided to William Allingham. By May Alexander Gilchrist had heard that some of the translations were appearing in the form of a printed book and he therefore assumed that the work had gone to Macmillan. If not, he advised Gabriel to send it directly to Henrietta Street and then to expect to wait a fortnight for the publisher to reach a definite decision. In the end, the book was brought out instead by Smith and Elder, chiefly because Ruskin undertook to pay part of the cost of publication.[1]

At any rate, beginning in 1861 Gabriel took steps to secure publication for both his own and his sister's work. *The Cornhill Magazine,* under Thackeray's editorship, had started in 1860, some few months after the appearance of the first number of *Macmillan's Magazine* in November, 1859. Although apparently Gabriel was unsuccessful in getting his own poems

---

[1] Letter of May 21, 1861, from Alexander Gilchrist to D. G. Rossetti, University of Texas MSS. For complete details of publication, see William E. Fredeman, "Bibliographical Notes & Queries," *The Book Collector* (Summer, 1961), pp. 193–198.

into *The Cornhill,* he asked Ruskin, then his patron, to "say a good word for something of Christina's to *Cornhill.*"

She had by then written *Up-hill* (1858) and *Goblin Market* (1859). Ruskin was the first person outside the immediate family to see what Gabriel called her "Poem about the two Girls and the Goblins." While he was shaking his head disapprovingly over this bizarre piece, Gabriel showed Macmillan *Up-hill.* The publisher was impressed. "I saw Macmillan last night," Gabriel wrote Christina, "who has been congratulated by some of his contributors on having got a poet at last in your person, and read aloud your lively little Song of the Tomb [*Up-hill*] with great satisfaction. He is anxious to see something else of yours, and is a man able to judge for himself; so I think you might probably do at least as well with him as with Masson. I told him of the poem Ruskin has, and he would like to see it if it does not go into *Cornhill.*" Macmillan likewise inquired whether Christina had much ready in manuscript, and Gabriel assured him there was a great deal of poetry available. Again Gabriel wrote to his sister, telling her that if she would set to it immediately and make a collected copy of her poems in printing form, he believed they would have a chance with Macmillan. In any case, they were "so unusually excellent, that there could be little doubt ever of their finding a publisher, not to speak of a public."

Shortly afterwards his ardor was dampened by receiving from Ruskin a negative verdict on *Goblin Market.* "It is with very great regret and disgust," he wrote William, "that I enclose a note from Ruskin about Christina's poems—most senseless, I think." The note is as follows:

DEAR ROSSETTI,

I sate up till late last night reading poems. They are full of beauty and power. But no publisher—I am deeply grieved to know this—would take them, so full are they of quaintnesses and other offences. Irregular measure (introduced to my great regret in its chief wilfullness by Coleridge) is the calamity of modern poetry. The *Iliad,* the *Divina Commedia,* the *Aenid,* the whole of Spenser, Milton, Keats, are written without taking a single license or violating the common ear for metre; your sister should exercise herself in the severest commonplace of metre until she can write as the public likes. Then if she puts in her observation and passion all will become precious. But she must have the Form first. . . .[2]

Still with his eye on Thackeray's magazine, Gabriel next thought of sending *Goblin Market* to William Allingham or to Mrs. Gaskell, who being "good-natured and appreciative," might get it into *The Cornhill*.

In the end it was Alexander Macmillan who rescued the poem from threatened oblivion. Despite his partiality for smoothness of rhythm and metrical regularity, he had what Charles Morgan calls "the boldness and imagination to take risks." Not the man to be daunted by something new and unfamiliar in poetry, he published *Up-hill* promptly in the February, 1861, issue of the magazine, and had Masson schedule *A Birthday* for April and *An Apple Gathering* for August publication. By October he had decided to bring out *Goblin Market* as the leading poem in a volume designed to catch the Christmas trade, writing to Gabriel on the 28th,

I was hoping to have seen you one of these Thursdays to talk about your sister's poems. I quite think a selection of them would have a chance—or to put it more truly that with some omissions they might do. At least I would run the risk of a small edition, with the two designs which you kindly offer.

My idea is to make an exceedingly pretty little volume, and to bring it out as a small Christmas book. This would give it every chance of coming right to the public. If the public prove a wise and discerning public and take a great fancy to it, we could soon give them an adequate supply.

The attraction of the volume would be the *Goblin Market,* and this I think should furnish any designs. But we must, of course, leave that to you. If you would be so good as to look in next Thursday, I would go over the poems and indicate what seems to me needful to be left out.

---

[2] William Michael Rossetti, ed., *Ruskin: Rossetti: PreRaphaelitism* (1899), pp. 258–259.

I enclose a rough specimen of the sort of style I thought of printing it in.

I took the liberty of reading the *Goblin Market* aloud to a number of people belonging to a small working-man's society here [Cambridge]. They seemed at first to wonder whether I was making fun of them; by degrees they got as still as death, and when I finished there was a tremendous burst of applause. I wish Miss Rossetti could have heard it.

A quaint wood-cut initial—not elaborate and not sprawling down the page, but with a queer goblin, say, grinning at a sweet, patient woman face—or something else of the kind would make a nice addition.[3]

By January of 1862 *Goblin Market* was in the press and by March it was published. Although Sir Edmund Gosse would have us believe that the book was the explosive bomb that blew up the beautifully guarded, velvet-lawned Tennysonian preserve, scattering into limbo the poets Gosse compares to gently grazing fallow deer and discreet thrushes—in other words that Christina's "brilliant, fantastic, and profoundly original volume . . . in 1862 . . . achieved the earliest popular success for Pre-Raphaelite poetry,"—in actuality the work was slow to catch hold, and as we can see by Christina's letters to Macmillan in 1863, it did not go into a second edition until 1865. F. T. Palgrave (Macmillan published his *Golden Treasury* in 1861) tried to get Tennyson to write a notice of the volume for *The Saturday Review* or *The London Review,* but although the laureate read Christina's poems "with pleasure," he refused to commit himself in print. The reviews as a whole were favorable, however, and even enthusiastic, although some of the reviewers seemed to be more taken by Gabriel's designs than by Christina's poetry.

That Macmillan was willing to hazard his and Daniel's hard-earned capital on the book was in itself a triumph, for fond as he was of good poetry, as a businessman he had to estimate its selling value. He once told Caroline Norton that

---

[3] George Macmillan, ed., *Letters of Alexander Macmillan* (Glasgow, privately printed, 1908), pp. 94–95.

according to Masson's figures, there were "some 20,000 of her Majesty's subjects in these islands who write verse more or less respectably," and to Thomas Berry he granted that "no inconsiderable number have to a high degree the gift of utterance in that line." But—and the but is a big one—"the point where that utterance is so imbued with genius that it will command a sale, is rather a nice thing to determine." Out of hundreds of such manuscripts that had passed through his hands (he was writing in October, 1862), he had published two, and "neither had succeeded commercially, though the merit really appeared to me very high in both cases." The question was, and still is, who among the rhythmically articulate deserves to be heard. "I tell you," he said with earnest emphasis, "I have frequently sent back what I felt to be beautiful and touching in verse, simply because I knew it would not sell. That is my business, to calculate what will commercially pay. Unless it will there is no reason why it should be printed."

His business, as he saw it, did not include the writing of literature. He himself, he insisted with undue modesty, was really "only a dealer in literature as any one might be in cheese or pork." He disclaimed any pretension to writing, either in poetry or prose. As Falstaff was the cause of wit in others, he said, so he was "the cause and origin of many books," although himself not a creator of them. Nevertheless, as Morgan pointed out, his was a unique function. Writers, like seamen, need to take their bearings, and a great publisher gives his authors that assurance which frequently must turn into reassurance. "In gigantic, honest letters, to chosen and rejected alike," writes Morgan, "he discussed men's work as they would have it discussed."

At the time Alexander began to publish the Rossettis, he himself read almost everything submitted to the firm. "My work is sometimes a little heavy," he admitted, "but I get on. The strain on one's mind as to what will answer and what will not is perhaps that which takes most out of one. Reading MSS., not for amusement, but with an eye to results, is heavier work than one would think at first sight. Not one in ten of what anyone reads appears, but one must do one's work wherever placed, and be thankful to have it to do."

As the following correspondence reveals, the three Rossettis were even more thankful to have the man Christina called "the staunch Mac" at the other end of the manuscript doing his work in his quiet and unobtrusive way.

THE LETTERS

1861–1864

The chief interest in this first group of letters is focused upon Dante Gabriel Rossetti's endeavor to get Alexander Macmillan to publish Swinburne's *Chastelard* and his *Poems and Ballads*. Some of the letters concern the reviews and presentation copies of Alexander Gilchrist's *Blake* (1863), to which the Rossetti brothers contributed, aiding Anne Gilchrist to complete the work upon her husband's death. William Rossetti's letters deal with Macmillan's publication of his blank verse translation of Dante's *Inferno* (1865), and Christina's with the publisher's proposal to bring out a second edition of *Goblin Market* and his suggestion that she produce a new volume of poetry.

1 ◇ *Christina Rossetti to Alexander Macmillan*

[December, 1861] [1]

My dear Mr. Macmillan

I have kept in mind that you did not approve of my photograph sent you a while ago: So now I have pleasure in offering you in exchange for it a carte just now taken, and reckoned here at home an excellent likeness.[2] Is it troubling you too much to ask you kindly to send me back whichever of the two you reject? one is so often asked for one's photograph that every copy has its value.

So near Christmas, allow me to offer you and yours all its best wishes.

Very truly yours

Christina G. Rossetti

45 Upper Albany St.
Wednesday morning.

---

[1] According to internal evidence, the month is December. I date the letter 1861 because with the publication of *Goblin Market* in the spring of 1862 Macmillan would have requested a photograph of the author before rather than ten months after publication.

[2] William Rossetti informs us that shortly before Christina went to France with him and their mother in the summer of 1861, three carte-de-visite photographs were taken of her (Memoir to the *Works,* p. liii, No. 22). Macmillan might have rejected one of these three, all of which William considered "extremely good," displaying to advantage the dignity and elegance of Christina's appearance.

My dear Mr. Macmillan

I received this morning a note from the Rev^d. Orby Shipley asking permission to republish in a *Lyra* (about November or December next) some of the Devotional pieces from my volume. I have already sent him three short unpublished pieces for the same purpose.[1] Will you favour me by letting me know whether my compliance with his request is likely in any degree to injure the sale of your edition[2] (I know not which nor how many pieces he would select)—because on this entirely depends my answering yes or no.

Pray pardon my troubling you for advice on a point which very likely does not affect you at all, and can seem of importance only to a person small in the literary world as I am.

Pardon also the extra scrawlings of my letter, as I cannot hold my pen well.

Yours always faithfully

Christina G. Rossetti

2nd July 1863
45 Upper Albany St. N.W.

Mrs. Gilchrist[3] tells me you have quitted Cambridge.[4] Am I still to direct to you there? or where?
P. S. Of course what I give to Mr. Shipley, I give: I do not receive money, and have no interest in the affair one way or the other.

---

[1] The Reverend Orby Shipley (1832–1916), author of *Tracts for the Day* (1868), edited three anthologies of religious poetry, the *Lyra Eucharistica* (1863), the *Lyra Messianica* (1864), and the *Lyra Mystica* (1865). All three contain Christina's poems. For the first edition of the *Lyra Eucharistica* Shipley selected two of the three poems Christina sent him. They are *The Offering of the New Law* (*Works*, p. 233) and *I Will Lift Up Mine Eyes to the Hills* (p. 184). In 1875 Macmillan published Shipley's *A Theory about Sin*.

[2] *Goblin Market* (March, 1862).

[3] Anne Gilchrist (1828–1885), widow of Alexander Gilchrist, author

of the *Life of Blake*. William Rossetti and Mrs. Gilchrist, admirer of Walt Whitman, became warm friends during their collaboration on Blake's *Life,* and in the summer of 1863 she invited Christina to visit her at Brookbank, Surrey. There, in the same house in which George Eliot wrote most of *Middlemarch,* Christina wrote *Maiden Song* (*Works,* p. 38), the poem Gladstone repeated by heart at a social function. See Herbert Gilchrist, *The Life and Letters of Anne Gilchrist* (1887).

[4] In 1863 AM removed the firm's headquarters to London, leaving his nephew, Robert Bowes, in charge of the Cambridge branch, which in time became the retail bookselling business of Bowes & Bowes. "I am now a Cockney by habitation," AM wrote his friend Alexander Geikie, the geologist, "having with much reluctance decided that London must now be my headquarters and Cambridge a branch. I have brought all my publishing staff with Mr. Fraser at its head, up to London. . . ." The same year AM became Oxford University's official publisher. He anticipated a busy summer: "I will be engaged in digging—not stones or fossils," he wrote Geikie, "but bricks and preparation for very 'recent formations.' I am about to make a house for myself for the business, and the building will occupy my summer" (*Macm. Lttrs.,* Glasgow ed., p. 145).

3 ❖ *W. M. Rossetti to Alexander Macmillan*

45 Upper Albany St. N.W.
7 Aug. [1863]

Dear Mr. Macmillan,

Some years ago I <wrote> began a translation of Dante's Commedia, & completed the Inferno, with the minimum of notes I thought requisite; & I am now minded to publish it.[1]

Having aforetime made one or two essays with Publishers which proved abortive, I don't intend now to trouble any one else, or myself, in like manner, but simply to publish the book on my own account,[2] fully persuaded that Publishers who fight shy of speculating in such wares are wise in their generation. Would it suit you to become the Publisher on this footing? [3] If so, I would gladly confide the M.S. to you in due course—which would be as soon as I have had time to give it a final revision.

I suppose the ordinary size for a small book—such as Christina's volume or a trifle larger—would be suitable.

She is in the country, or would, I am sure, join me in cordial remembrances.

Very faithfully yours,

W. M. Rossetti

---

[1] Marginal note by the firm, written above the address: "Wrote from Sandown Aug. 11. saying we would gladly publish this for him."

[2] William's mother, Frances Lavinia Rossetti (1800–1886), paid the cost of publication (£50). Despite his duties at the Inland Revenue Office, William had worked on the translation for some nine years. His avowed aim was "a direct literal and unmodified rendering of what Dante said." In the 1860's there were three acceptable translations of the *Inferno* in English: Henry Francis Cary's in blank verse, Charles Bagot Cayley's in *terza rima* (see below, Lttr. 99, n. 3), and John Carlyle's in prose. Shortly after William's book appeared, Longfellow published his blank verse translation, likewise aiming at literal exactness. "Of all men, I am the one whom it would least beseem to debate which of the two versions is the more successful," William commented, adding, however, that Longfellow took liberties he would not allow himself (*Remin.*, II, 308–310). See also below, Lttr. 25 and n. 1.

[3] Morgan, in his history of the firm, says that an author who persuades a great house to publish for him on commission is fortunate: "in fact, the Macmillans, and all other publishers of repute, avoid this form of contract unless there is exceptional reason for it" (pp. 108–109).

4 ❖ *D. G. Rossetti to Alexander Macmillan*

14 Oct 1863

16 Cheyne Walk

Chelsea [1]

My dear Macmillan

As I see the *Blake* announced for this week, I write in hope that you may consider my brother's & my joint contributions [2] to it worthy of 3 copies (in addition to the one I already have in sheets.) Two would be for ourselves & the 3rd I purpose giving to Munro,[3] who says that if I name him it may incline you all the more to comply.

If you are ever my way here I shall be very happy indeed to see you and am always

Yours sincerely

DG Rossetti

A Macmillan Esq

---

[1] DGR leased Tudor House in Chelsea in 1862, and from then on his writing paper shows the Cheyne Walk letterhead with the engraved design of two contiguous circles, one with the motto, *"Frangas non Flectas."* William Rossetti, Swinburne, and Meredith were his subtenants during the 1860's.

[2] Alexander Gilchrist, *Life of William Blake, "Pictor Ignotis,"* two vols. (1863). Gabriel edited Blake's unpublished poetry in the second volume, wrote a supplementary chapter to the *Life,* and filled in the blank pages in the chapter on the *Inventions to the Book of Job.* William annotated the catalogue of Blake's pictures and drawings, and inserted some critical remarks in the *Life.* Mrs. Gilchrist in her preface calls their contributions "a labor of love." See above, Lttr. 2, n. 3.

[3] Alexander Munro (1825–1871), the sculptor, was an Inverness man who came to London under the patronage of the Duke and Duchess of Sutherland. Macmillan mentions him in a letter of 1860 as one of the brilliant circle of artistic, literary, and scientific men who frequented his Thursday evening "Tobacco Parliaments."

5 ❖ *W. M. Rossetti to Alexander Macmillan*

16 Cheyne Walk

Chelsea

29 Oct [1863]

Dear Mr. Macmillan,

We are much obliged for the Blakes: tho' tolerably familiar with it, I shall enjoy a "good read" of my copy in its complete state.

I am sorry to trouble you about the enclosed copy: but, if you will look at vol. 1, you will find sheet X 2 repeated, & in vol. 2 the more serious error that, after p. 240, what follows is the pages proper to vol. 1, not 2. May I trouble you to have this rectified in whatever is the fittest manner, & then to transmit the copy direct to

Capt. Butts [1]

Army & Navy Club.

————

My brother suggests to me this opportunity of reminding you of your kind proposal of letting each of us have an extra copy—of course only when quite convenient to you. He also suggests that, either from yourself or from us (according to what you were so good as to say of further copies), it might be well to send the book to Mr. Allingham,[2] (Customs, Lymington, [Hants]), who has done something for Blake, & is mentioned in the book, to Mr. Swinburne [3] (address same as our own) who has been of some real service throughout the work, & to Robert Browning (19 Warwick Crescent, Hanover Road) one of whose poems suggested the title Pictor Ignotus,[4] & who is greatly interested in Blake, & desirous of being of service to the book.

Yours very truly,

W. M. Rossetti

————

[1] The grandson of Thomas Butts, Blake's life-long friend and patron. Captain Butts made the Blake-Butts correspondence available to William.

[2] William Allingham (1824–1889), the Irish poet, said to have influenced Yeats. After some years as a customs official at Lymington, he became assistant editor and subsequently editor of *Fraser's Magazine* (1870–1879). See *Letters of Dante Gabriel Rossetti to William Allingham, 1854–70,* ed. G. B. Hill (1897).

[3] In 1862 the Rossettis consulted Swinburne about his undertaking a revision of Blake's *Prophetic Books.* Swinburne replied it was useless to attempt to patch or pad out the book, "even if one's patchwork were to come under no further supervision from a chaste publisher. . . . It seems to me that the best thing for the book and for those interested in it is to leave it alone, for fear of bursting the old bottles—a Scotch publisher would no doubt receive a reference to the sacred text as unanswerable. I should have been delighted to help in

18

the work originally, and coming in as a free auxiliary to the best of my means of work; but I see no good possible to do at this point, even if one disliked less the notion of doing service for Blake under the eye of such a taskmaster as the chaste Macmillan" (Lang, I, 59–60). Swinburne's most notable contribution to Blake studies is *William Blake, a Critical Essay* (1868).

[4] The lines from Browning's *Pictor Ignotus* quoted in Gilchrist's *Life* are as follows:

> The sanctuary's gloom at least shall ward
> Vain tongues from where my pictures stand apart.

Although Macmillan admired Browning, he was not always sure what the poet was up to. He described *Mr. Sludge, the Medium* and *Bishop Blougram* as "a nice, somewhat peculiar pair," but confessed to Browning that a single reading of *Caliban* was "enough for a dull fellow." Assuring the poet that he "somewhat guessed the drift," he added, "But you do read us riddles. 'Doth he not speak in parables?' Still we are thankful he does speak" (*Macm. Lttrs.*, Glasgow ed., p. 178).

6 ✧ *Christina Rossetti to Alexander Macmillan*

My dear Mr. Macmillan

I enclose my receipt and many thanks for the cheque— and many more thanks for the kind words of encouragement you give me. Miss Proctor [1] I am not afraid of: but Miss Ingelow [2] (judging by extracts; I have not yet seen the actual volume)—would be a formidable rival to most men, and to any woman. Indeed I have been bewailing that she did not publish with you.

Few things within the range of probability would give me greater pleasure than to <hand> see in print my second volume: but I am sadly convinced that I have not by me materials, equal both in quantity and quality, to what are already before the public. And, if one conviction can go beyond another, I am yet more firmly convinced that my system of not writing against the grain is the right one, at any rate as concerns myself. Had a second edition of *Goblin Market* been called for, one considerably augmented would have been at

once feasible: but a second volume must I fear stand over
to the indefinite future.

Yours very truly

Christina G. Rossetti

45 Upper Albany St. N. W.

1st December [1863]

6A ENCLOSURE: *Christina Rossetti
to Alexander Macmillan*

London 1st December 1863.

Received of Alexander Macmillan Esqu. the sum of three
pounds three shillings for *One Day*.[3]

Christina G. Rossetti

£3-3-0

---

[1] Adelaide Proctor (1825–1864), a popular poet of the day, is now
chiefly remembered for her song, "The Lost Chord." In 1882 John H.
Ingram asked Christina to write Miss Proctor's biography for his
Eminent Women series. She considered it, but finally decided that
she had "so long dropped out of literary society that I mistrust my
ability to get at private sources of information." See below, Lttr. 112,
n. 2.

[2] Jean Ingelow (1820–1897) had caused a stir in the literary world
with her first published volume of poems. "What think you of Jean
Ingelow, the wonderful poet?" Christina inquired of Dora Greenwell
in a frequently quoted letter of December 31, 1863. "I have not yet read
the volume, but reviews with copious extracts have made me aware
of a new eminent name having arisen among us. I want to know who
she is, what she is like, where she lives. . . ." (Bell, p. 161). Some
years later in criticizing Christina's *The Lowest Room* (*Works,* p. 16),
Gabriel attributed its tone of "falsetto muscularity" to Miss Ingelow's
influence, but Christina replied that the poem had been written long
before she knew Miss Ingelow, and therefore "Miss J.I. could not
have mis-led me any-whither." (*Fam. Lttrs.,* p. 55.) See below, Lttr.
31, n. 3.

[3] *Works,* p. 330.

20

7 ❖ *W. M. Rossetti to Alexander Macmillan*

Inland Revenue Office
Somerset House, W. C.
21 Jan. [1864] [1]

Dear Mr. Macmillan,

My brother asked me last night to drop you a note on the following point.

You may remember that one of the persons to whom it was proposed to send a copy of the Blake was Capt. Butts, grandson of Blake's friend Butts, & contributor of the letters we published in vol. 2, also that a copy was sent for him to us at Chelsea, but which proved to be imperfect, & was returned to you, when you were so good as to say that you would substitute another, & send it to Capt. Butts. Now the Capt. happened to call yesterday on my brother, & it turns out that the book never reached him. Perhaps you would kindly look into this. His address is

Salterns
Parkstone
Dorset
Yours truly,
W. M. Rossetti

---

[1] I date this letter by a marginal note: "Sent Jan 25. 64."

8 ❖ *D. G. Rossetti to Alexander Macmillan*

[March] 1864 [1]

My dear Macmillan

I have been wishing to write to you respecting the poems of my friend Mr. Swinburne, of which you have I think already heard something both from me and others— They are still unpublished, their author being more apt to write new ones than to think of the old. I hardly know how to give you an adequate idea of what not I alone, but many excellent judges who have seen them, think of their astonishing beauty. They inspire a certainty that Swinburne, who is still very young, is destined to take in his own generation the acknowledged place which Tennyson holds among his contemporaries. I should like you much to be the first to have submitted to you the work which both Swinburne and I think the best adapted to come first before the public. It is a tragedy on the subject of Chastelard and Mary Queen of Scots. If you have time at present for consideration of it, will you let me know, and it shall be sent to you at once.

With Kind Remembrances

    I am,

    my dear Macmillan,

Ever yours truly,

DG Rossetti

A Macmillan Esq

---

[1] The top of this letter is torn off so that the date reads "rch 1864."

9 ❖ *Christina Rossetti to Alexander Macmillan*

Mrs. Austin—51 Rue D'Amsterdam—Paris [1]

My dear Mr. Macmillan

If, as I think, one of my little M.S. books is still in your hands, may I ask you obligingly to let me have it back, as I really want it for use.[2]

Yours very truly

Christina G. Rossetti

45 Upper Albany St. N. W.

4th April [1864] [3]

---

[1] Marginal note not in CGR's handwriting. I do not identify Mrs. Austin.

[2] CGR wrote and dated her poems in seventeen manuscript notebooks from 1842 to 1866. Nine are in the Bodleian Library, Oxford (Don 3 1/9), seven in the Ashley Library at the British Museum (Ash.

1362 and 1364), and one in the possession of CGR's grand-niece, Mrs. Imogene Rossetti Dennis. The latter (March 21, 1859 to December 31, 1860) contains the holograph MS of *Goblin Market*.

[3] For conjectural dating of this and the following three letters (9–12) see Lttr. 12, n. 1.

10 ◈ *Christina Rossetti to Alexander Macmillan*

45 Upper Albany St. N. W. [April] 8th [1864]
My dear Mr. Macmillan

I received my little book quite safely, thank you.

I am in great hopes of being able to put a volume together, and will see about it;—indeed some calculation of length, etc., already made point in the right direction. Mr. Masson has 2 little things of mine in hand, and you may think whether I am not happy to attain fame (!) and guineas by means of the Magazine.[1]

Yours very truly
Christina G. Rossetti

---

[1] Macmillan started his magazine November, 1859, as an "experiment of a popular shilling monthly with some new features." David Masson (1822–1907) was its first editor, a position he held from 1859 to 1865, when he was appointed professor of English Literature at Edinburgh University. Among his more important literary contributions were his biographies of Milton and De Quincey, and his editions of their works.

Christina's "2 little things" which the magazine published that year are *The Lowest Room* (*Works*, p. 16, see above, Lttr. 6, n. 2), which appeared in the March, 1864, issue, and *My Friend* (*Works*, p. 336) in December.

11 ◈ *Christina Rossetti to Alexander Macmillan*

[June, 1864]
My dear Mr. Macmillan

I enclose my receipt for half profits:[1] with my grateful

thanks, as I am sure I could have no sort of claim upon them when you alone ran the risk.

Of course I shall delight in 2nd edition of *Goblin Market*. About possible vol. 2. I will write again, please, in a few days; meanwhile am sincerely gratified at what you say so kindly.

Yours very truly
Christina G. Rossetti

45 Upper Albany St. N. W.
Wednesday

---

[1] The system of half-profits used by Macmillan was considered advantageous to both author and publisher. If a book succeeded, the publisher reaped the golden profit; if it failed, the author lost nothing thereby, since the publisher assumed the risk of production costs (Morgan, p. 109).

12 ❖ *Christina Rossetti to Alexander Macmillan*

45 Upper Albany St. N. W.
Wednesday [1864] [1]

My dear Mr. Macmillan

I have weighed and measured, but alas! vol. 2 is not ready. Pray pardon my delay in letting you know this, but I only today arrived at this final conclusion.

Hoping for a different result some day
Sincerely yours,
Christina G. Rossetti

---

[1] It is possible to date this group of letters by a letter William printed in the *Rossetti Papers* (p. 50) which is dated May 7, 1864. "Don't think me a perfect weathercock," Christina wrote Gabriel, "But why rush before the public with an immature volume? I really think of not communicating at all with Mac at present; but waiting the requisite number of months (or years as the case may be) until I have a sufficiency of quality as well as quantity. Is not this after all the best plan? If meanwhile my things become remains, that need be no bugbear to scare me into premature publicity. . . ."

13 ❖ D. G. Rossetti to Alexander Macmillan

Wednesday [1864]
16 Cheyne Walk
Chelsea

My dear Macmillan,

Pardon my not thanking you before for the interesting catalog by Count Mortara,[1] whom I remember at my father's house in my boyhood. It being dated for this year, I judge he must still be living. When you can, I shall be glad to hear from you, as I said in my last, anent Swinburne's poetry. I have forgotten till now to thank you for the introduction to the Revᵈ. Mr. Blunt,[2] who seems quite an exceptionally first-rate fellow.

Yours ever sincerely
DG Rossetti

A Macmillan Esq

---

[1] Both the Cavalier Mortara and his brother, the Conte Mortara, a prominent bibliophile, were frequent visitors at the Rossetti home at 50 Charlotte Street during Gabriel's childhood.

[2] ? John Henry Blunt (1823–1884), author of the *Annotated Book of Common Prayer* (1866) and *The Book of Church Law* (1873). But Graves speaks of the Cambridge professor, W. C. Blunt, described by Dr. Sebastian Evans, AM's close friend, as "fiery and impulsive, but always kindly" (p. 106).

14 ❖ Alexander Macmillan to D. G. Rossetti
Text: *Macm. Lttrs.*, Glasgow ed., p. 172.

June 3, 1864

To D. G. Rossetti

I wanted very much to have read Swinburne's poem again carefully, and if possible aloud to my wife and sister-in-law. I certainly thought it a work of genius, but some parts of it were very queer—very. Whether the public could be expected to like them was doubtful. I will try and test it, in the way I have indicated, soon. Do you think he would send me the minor poems to look at? I could perhaps judge better of what a volume would be like.

15 ❖ *D. G. Rossetti to Alexander Macmillan*

29 June 1864
16 Cheyne Walk
Chelsea

My dear Macmillan

Will you kindly let me have an answer about Swinburne's "Chastelard." [1] I would also be glad to know from you whether you think that a volume of "Poems & Ballads" by him would be likely to suit you for publication. [2] They are no less than supremely splendid work.

With kind remembrances,

I am,

my dear Macmillan,

ever Sincerely yours
D.G. Rossetti

A. Macmillan Esq

---

[1] Some years later (1871) Macmillan confided to a correspondent that he was totally out of sympathy with Swinburne's interpretation of Mary Stuart, "carried to characteristically hideous exaggeration" (*Macm. Lttrs.*, Glasgow ed., pp. 262–263).

[2] Swinburne might have anticipated a rejection from "the chaste Macmillan," of whom Mrs. Gilchrist said, he "is far more inexorable against any shade of heteroxy in morals than in religion" (Lang, I, 59–60, n. 6).

16 ❖ *D. G. Rossetti to Alexander Macmillan*

[Summer, 1864] [1]

My dear Macmillan

My brother used to write on Art for the Saturday, but has not done so now for years.[2] As for myself, neither there nor in any other publication did I ever write a word on that subject, & it is the only subject on which I should make a principle of not writing—my business in connection with Art being to paint & not to write. Nor should I be competent without special study (for which I have no time) to write on the many branches of Italian literature involved in the Mortara catalogue— I did not hitherto understand that you had expressed a wish to see other poems of Swinburne but will now speak to him—

Yours ever truly
DG Rossetti

P. S. My brother is in Italy just now. I will show him the Catalogue on his return.

---

[1] The top of this letter is torn off, but DGR's postscript, referring to William's visit to Italy, establishes the date. According to his diary entries, William was in Italy from June 14 to July 14, 1864 (*Ross. Pprs.,* pp. 54–58).

[2] William was art critic for *The Saturday Review* for a short time in 1858 but was dismissed because his championship of the PreRaphaelite cause displeased Beresford Hope, the proprietor.

17 ❖ *D. G. Rossetti to Alexander Macmillan*

13 July [1864]
16 Cheyne Walk
Chelsea

My dear Macmillan

Swinburne will get together some of his poems and send them you. More anon—

Yours ever
DG Rossetti

18 ❖ *D. G. Rossetti to Alexander Macmillan*

24 Aug 1864
16 Cheyne Walk
Chelsea

My dear Macmillan

If you're disposed for a really well done review of the *Blake*,[1] would you send a copy to the *Edinburgh Courant*, of which my friend James Hannay is editor.[2] He is quite an old Blakian, & would do it himself but never got the book when published. With kind remembrances
I am yours ever truly

DG Rossetti

I shall be sending you Swinburne's poetry immediately

---

[1] Macmillan wrote James MacLehose November, 1863, "See how well the *Blake* is being reviewed. There will be a good many more important notices. We have sold about 500. As nobody knew about Blake, and the book had its way to fight, this is not bad. It goes on daily selling too" (*Macm. Lttrs.*, Glasgow ed., p. 159). Morgan states that the publication of this work, "for which at the time there was no obvious public," was responsible for rescuing Blake from oblivion (p. 71).

[2] James Hannay (1827–1873) was one of those brilliant eccentrics cherished in the Rossetti circle. Originally a Navy man, he turned to literature and journalism, writing two three-volume novels, a collection of sea tales, and the notes for Thackeray's *English Humourists* (1853) before he became editor of *The Edinburgh Courant* (1860–1864). His edition of Edgar Allan Poe's *Poems* (1853) was dedicated to D. G. Rossetti.

19 ❧ D. G. Rossetti to Alexander Macmillan

5 Sept. 1864
16 Cheyne Walk
Chelsea

My dear Macmillan

Herewith by Book Post you have a supply of Swinburne's miscellaneous poems. Would you kindly let me know that you get them safely. I know your address is changed but always forget the new one.[1]

Yours very truly
DG Rossetti

A Macmillan Esq

---

[1] 16 Bedford Street, Covent Garden, from 1863 to 1873.

20 ❧ D. G. Rossetti to Alexander Macmillan

7 Sept 1864
16 Cheyne Walk
Chelsea

My dear Macmillan

I am not quite sure of being in town on Tuesday next, but if so will certainly be at Vic. Street: at 5—45, with thanks to you for lugging me out— If I'm not there you'll know I left town.

Yours ever
DG Rossetti

21 ❖ *D. G. Rossetti to Alexander Macmillan*

[Sept., 1864]
16 Cheyne Walk
Chelsea

My dear Macmillan

I have just got Swinburne's M.S.S. from No. 5 where they have been left.[1] I will make a choice of those which seem to me feasible, & let you have them again for second thoughts. I hope to see you Saturday with all the ladies who can [illegible] you to come so far. I'm doing a Venus;[2] which I mean to make a stunner.

In haste
ever yours
DGR

---

[1] I do not identify No. 5. Swinburne was in Cornwall during the autumn of 1864.
[2] The *Venus Verticordia*, listed as No. 198 in the third edition of H. C. Marillier, *Dante Gabriel Rossetti* (1899).

22 ❖ *W. M. Rossetti to Alexander Macmillan*

45 Upper Albany St. N. W.
9 Sept. [1864]

Dear Macmillan,

The print is exactly such as I like.[1] The size should, I think, be a trifle larger—such as indicated in 2nd page: you will understand how to construe the proposal there made. The space between the lines is rather ample. If a slight diminution of it (besides the greater number of lines dependent on increased size of paper) would make any difference worth considering in the total cost for paper; I would like it adopted, as I must keep the expense down as far as reasonable. You will perceive whether or not it is worth while, & please order accordingly. The large print shown on p. 4 should, I think, be confined to preface only—all other introductory matter being on p. 3.

With thanks & waiting to see you Tuesday, Yours very truly,

W. M. Rossetti.

---

[1] *Macmillan's Bibliographical Catalogue* lists the work (1864) as *The Comedy of Dante Allighieri, Part i—The Hell.* Translated into Blank Verse by William Michael Rossetti, with introduction and Notes. According to William's statements and supporting evidence, the translation was published in February, 1865 (*Ross. Pprs.,* p. ix; *Remin.,* II, 308. See also below, Lttrs. 25, n. 1, and 36).

23 ❖ *D. G. Rossetti to Swinburne*
Text: Lang, I, 108 (reproduced in part below).

16 Cheyne Walk, Chelsea
September 15, 1864

My dear Swinburne,

Mac has spoken. Don't swear more than you can help. I have your M.S.S. safe again. There was a sort of talk of my looking up and putting together those against which there could be no possible objection in reason and sending them him again. He seems half inclined to the Chastelard still. But I since doubted whether such selection would meet your wishes. I mentioned the St. Dorothy as an unobjectionable poem, but Mac had some funky reminiscences of the allusions to Venus, so really it seemed a bad lookout. . . .

24 ❖ *Christina Rossetti to Alexander Macmillan*

My dear Mr. Macmillan

Thank you for kindly offering us a second time colour-patterns for the binding: but if your taste coincided with Gabriel's and my own, I think you could hardly select a more

31

becoming shade for my Goblins than the fine red in which you have dressed Mr. Allingham's ballad book.[1]

I suppose Gabriel may be at Chelsea again by the end of next week;[2] but as this my brother has either never been reduced to rule, or else as I am not mistress of the rule whereby to calculate him, I can but throw out my suggestion as based on his last letter home.

Your often obliged
Christina G. Rossetti

45 Upper Albany St. N. W.
17th November [1864].

---

[1] It will be seen that Macmillan was going ahead with the second edition of *Goblin Market,* illustrated by Gabriel's woodcuts. The color finally selected was dark blue. Allingham's *Ballad Book* was originally suggested by AM, who published it in 1864 as part of the *Golden Treasury* series.

[2] DGR was in Paris during November, returning to Chelsea before November 24 (*Ross. Pprs.,* p. 65).

25 ❖ W. M. Rossetti to Alexander Macmillan

Somerset House.
29 Nov. [1864]

Dear Macmillan,

I'm sorry to bother you, or to appear (possibly) fussy: but I think your printer's pace is rather too slavishly imitative of a snail's. It is, I think, 4 weeks or even more since I received a single new proof (revises not reckoned); & at this rate the better part of next year might be gone before the book comes out. This I should not wish, & know no reason for. Also it happens that an acquaintance of yours, the Rev^d. Prebendary Ford, is bringing out a terza rima Inferno with Smith & Elder: &, tho' I have a very high opinion of the translation & wish it every conceivable success, I should not desire to see it out before mine—which was in the printer's hands a couple of months or so earlier.[1]

Would you give him a gentle prod, please, if it is your business; or let me know that it is mine, & I will officiate.

Yours truly,

W. M. Rossetti

---

[1] William's *Inferno* did beat Ford's to the draw. It was out and ready for distribution by February 26, 1865 (see below, Lttr. 36), whereas Smith and Elder had only got around to announcing Ford's translation—"in the Metre of the Original"—in *The Athenæum* March 18. The Reverend James A. Ford (1797–1877) was Prebendary of Exeter.

26 ❖ Christina Rossetti to Alexander Macmillan

81 High St. Hastings

Wednesday [Dec., 1864] [1]

My dear Mr. Macmillan

I expect to remain here for the rest of the Winter very likely, so will you kindly let me have my proofs at this address.

It's rather early for Christmas wishes, yet lest I should not write again in time I venture now to offer my very cordial best wishes to Mrs. Macmillan and all your family.

Very truly yours

Christina G. Rossetti

My Mother charges me with her compliments.

---

[1] A chest ailment sent Christina to Hastings, where she remained from December, 1864, to April, 1865. Some years later she told F. G. Stephens that Hastings was "almost" her favorite spot in England. While there she wrote the long poem *Prince's Progress,* and put together the volume of which it is the title piece, her previously relinquished "vol. 2." She also wrote a number of notable lyrics at Hastings and corresponded almost daily with Gabriel about the contents and make-up of both the new volume and the second edition of *Goblin Market.*

27 ❖ Christina Rossetti to Alexander Macmillan

81 High Street, Hastings

20th [Dec., 1864]

My dear Mr. Macmillan

Thank you for kindly causing a letter directed to your care to reach me.

Said letter is from the Rev^d. R. H. Baynes, Editor of *Lyra Anglicana;* and asks my permission to reprint *From House to Home* [1] in *English Lyrics,* a volume which he is arranging for publication. As the object of publishing this volume is to promote a charitable <object> undertaking, I would at once yield my consent with all the good will in the world, only I should be glad first to be assured that my so doing is not likely to prejudice our 2nd edition. Will you kindly enlighten me on this point? If you deem the risk considerable, perhaps some shorter piece not yet in print may satisfy my Rev^d correspondent.

I hear that my *Echo* [2] is likely to be published, set to music by a Miss Gabriel.[3]

Yours very truly

Christina G. Rossetti

---

[1] *Works,* pp. 20–26. The poem was printed in *English Lyrics* (1865), pp. 109–118.

[2] *Works,* p. 314. Dorothy Stuart calls *Echo* "one of the most interesting of Christina's shorter lyrics, but likewise one of the hardest to interpret in the light of her personal history" (*Christina Rossetti,* E.M.L. series, 1930, p. 49). But as originally written in manuscript, the poem is much longer and more autobiographically revealing than in the printed version. For omitted stanzas, see *Christina Rossetti,* pp. 90–91.

[3] I do not identify her.

81 High St., Hastings
Monday [Dec., 1864]

My dear Mr. Macmillan

I am very glad to let Mr. Baynes have *From House to Home* and will write to him. The more of my things get set to music the better pleased I am, so of course I welcome Miss Smith.[1]

Always truly yours
Christina G. Rossetti

------

[1] "A Miss Smith [unidentified] has asked and obtained Mac's leave to melodize one of my things, I know not which," Christina wrote Gabriel. "The other day a Rev. Mr. Baynes wrote begging my permission for him to reprint *House to Home*, in a collection he is preparing to promote a charitable object: after consulting Mac I consented" (*Fam. Lttrs.*, p. 29).

1865

This group of letters is concerned chiefly with the publication of the second edition of *Goblin Market,* 1865, with Dante Gabriel's two woodcuts illustrating the volume, and with the preparation of Christina's *Prince's Progress* (1866), and the new volume Macmillan had been urging her to produce. Finished by May, when she went to Italy with William and their mother, and scheduled for 1865 publication, the book did not appear until a year later, owing to Dante Gabriel's delay in supplying the illustrations. Except for his dilatoriness in this one respect, he devoted himself during the year to furthering with single-minded enthusiasm his sister's career. He even attempted to regulate her business relations with Macmillan, but in so doing he muddled her affairs to such an extent that she finally had to tell him politely but firmly to keep hands off. The few letters from William are about his translation of the *Inferno.*

29 ❖ *Christina Rossetti to Alexander Macmillan*

81 High St. Hastings
7th [Jan.] 1865

My dear Mr. Macmillan

We reciprocate to you and yours very heartily all best wishes of the season.

I fear my proofs have become very tiresome to you through missing sheets; but indeed I well remember having, and cannot doubt that I returned, F: perhaps I forgot to mark it <u>Prep</u>, but hope this would not entail much extra trouble. Your speed is mine, as regards the date of issuing edition 2: but February sounds near and pleasant. Though I am likely to remain here for the rest of the Winter, please continue to send proofs to 166 Albany St.,[1] as by so doing they get the advantage of my sister's[2] revision as well as of my own.

As far as I can make it out from description and a scratch, I think Gabriel's design for the binding of William's *Dante* very effective.

Yours very truly
Christina G. Rossetti

---

[1] The Rossettis moved to Albany Street in 1854 and remained there until 1867. Originally the address had been No. 45 Upper Albany Street, but after several years was changed to No. 166 Albany Street. The house, a few doors from Christ Church, Albany Street (which Christina attended for almost twenty years), was demolished in 1960 to make way for the new parish school.

[2] Maria Francesca Rossetti (1827–1876). For further information about the relation between the two sisters, see my article, *PMLA*, p. 384, n. 2, and below, Lttr. 95, n. 2.

Turn over [1]

11 Jan
1865

My dear Macmillan

I've heard nothing, but <will> write with this to a man named Sachs of whom I know something, & ask him to fetch the block at yours and bring it on to me.

Mr. Burn called today on me & is about the cover.[2]

I was glad of the article on Christina, but, considering the high estimate, there might have been a line or two more.[3]

Ever yours

DG Rossetti

P.S. I do not know whether Sheet M of Goblin Market is yet finally reprinted.[4] If not, would you delay till you hear from my sister, as I am suggesting a <correction> change of a line to her.

P.S. I have a sketch for the *Prince's* binding somewhere which I'll send you. But please let me choose a colour. I think white's the best perhaps. It looks well in a cover I designed for Swinburne's *Atalanta*.[5]

---

[1] DGR's handwriting. Refers to the second P. S. on the back of the page.

[2] Macmillan's bookbinder. It is uncertain whether he was James Frederick (1794–1877) or his son James Robert Burn (1836–1905), probably the latter. Both appear in the records of the publishing house. Morgan says that Macmillan was greatly concerned with the details of book production and "gave precise instructions to the designers who worked for him" (p. 64).

[3] See below, Lttr. 31 and n. 3.

[4] See below, Lttr. 31, n. 2.

[5] *Atalanta,* finished in the autumn of 1864 (Lang, I, 115), was published the following March. DGR's white cover on the first edition still "looks well." Green was the color finally selected for *Prince's Progress*.

31 ⋄ *Christina Rossetti to Alexander Macmillan*

81 High Street

Hastings

14th [Jan., 1865]

Sheet M has not been printed.[1]

We are waiting. [Macm.]

My dear Mr. Macmillan

Should not 2nd edition be added to my title page?[2] I enclose my last proof to you in the doubt.

Of course sheet M has been printed off, so I will not trouble you on account of Gabriel's suggestion. How opportune just now the Times notice.[3]

Yours very truly,

Christina G. Rossetti

---

[1] Sheet M consisted of the poems *Sleep at Sea* (*Works*, pp. 154–156) and *From House to Home* (see above, Lttrs. 27 and 28). Although the firm's marginal note informs us that Sheet M had not yet been printed, on the sixteenth CGR wrote Gabriel that she did not think his "critique on sheet M can profit me this edition, as surely M must already be printed off; but thanks all the same. Foreseeing inutility, I have not grappled with the subject by comparing passages (N.B. Nerves)" (*Ross. Pprs.*, p. 73).

[2] It was. See below, Lttr. 33.

[3] "Modern Poets" appeared in *The Times*, January 11, 1865, p. 12. After disposing of Tennyson and Browning, the reviewer, Eneas Sweetland Dallas, considers "the young and rising brood of poets," discussing first the two foremost living women poets, Miss Jean Ingelow and Miss Christina Rossetti (see above, Lttr. 6 and n. 2). Miss Ingelow "is apt to be vague, and has not yet learned how to be brief." Although Miss Rossetti's work "has not yet received the same favour from the public," her art is "simpler, firmer, and deeper." Dallas concludes that Miss Ingelow is still "a child of promise," whereas Miss Rossetti's work is that of a finished artist. See *Christina Rossetti*, p. 194.

32 ❖ *D. G. Rossetti to Alexander Macmillan*

24 Jan 1865

My dear Macmillan

I'm quite vexed you should just have hit on one of the very few occasions on which I have slept from home— All the more that I ought to have written you before this.

The phenomenal stupidity of the fool who has plugged that block is enough to make one loathe one's kind. How the printer managed to print the whole 1st edition <with an apparent> so as to give the appearance of a gap in the block I cannot think. But from the first proof taken by this plugger (really there is a nautical rhyme to the word which one would like to use!) it became evident that the block was all right, whereupon, without consulting me at all, the beastly ass goes and cuts half a face out. I do not know whether I can set it right, but will see to it without fail today or tomorrow. I would have done so before but for much preoccupation. As soon as it is drawn, I will either send it at once to an engraver myself or send it to you for that purpose.

I hear no more from Burn, who has my full directions for William's binding.

Ever yours
DG Rossetti

33 ❖ *D. G. Rossetti to Alexander Macmillan*

3 Feb 1865
16 Cheyne Walk
Chelsea

My dear Macmillan

I hope the block will reach you quite finished on Tuesday or at the latest Wednesday next. There has been some trouble with it, and now I am having the words Second Edition [1] added in the vacant space originally left for them above the vignette. The engraver I am employing is Miss Faulkner, 35 Queen Square, Bloomsbury, whom I will ask to state her charge & let you know.[2]

Wells will also have a slight further charge for plugging the block for the words as above. The drawing is all right again now.

I have seen a frontispiece & vignette to Tom Taylor's Breton Ballads,[3] designed by Tissot, which are admirable things. Could you, as their publisher, let me have a proof of each separate from the work?

Ever yours
DG Rossetti

A Macmillan Esq

---

[1] See above, Lttr. 31.

[2] Possibly the sister of Charles Faulkner, member of the celebrated firm of Morris, Marshall, Faulkner, and Co. It was Faulkner who engraved the woodcut for Gabriel's frontispiece to the first edition of *Goblin Market*.

[3] Tom Taylor (1817–1880), popular playwright, critic, and editor of *Punch* from 1874 to 1880, translated the Ballads and Songs of Brittany from the "Barsaz-Breiz" of Vicomte Hersart de la Villemarqué. The work was published by Macmillan in 1866 "with some of the original melodies harmonised by Mrs. Tom Taylor with illustrations by J. Tissot, J. E. Millais, R. A. J. Tenniel, C. Keene, E. Borbould, and H. K. Browne" (*Macm. Cat.*, p. 141). Upon hearing of Taylor's death, Gabriel wrote his mother, "I knew him well some years ago. He seems lately to have had some sort of stroke, but wrote to the papers to say it was an attack of gout (in denial of their statement). However, he has corroborated them by dying, poor man! He was not always an unprejudiced critic, I think; but he was a man of many private charities, which will miss him sorely" (*DGRFL*, II, 361).

<10> 11 Feb 1865
16 Cheyne Walk
Chelsea

My dear Macmillan

Here at last is the *Goblin Market* block, all right as regards
Miss Faulkner's (the engraver's work), for which will you
please send her what is right to her address 35 <u>Queen Square</u>
<u>W.C.</u> She has had a good deal of trouble but I cannot get her
to name a charge. I should think £2 would be right. She is
a professional engraver, & I could not have thought of going
to her unless with the idea that she would accept payment, as
you mentioned your willingness to pay necessary expenses.

She tells me that the plug is not quite perfect in the vignette,
but is likely unless very carefully printed, to show a white
line. Will you let me have a first proof or two that I may
attend to this & the general printing which was very bad in
the 1st edition.

Yours ever
DG Rossetti

Burn has finished my brother's binding all right. I hope Christina is now really getting a new volume in line, having got a
longish first poem.[1]

---

[1] *Prince's Progress.* On December 23 Christina wrote Gabriel from
Hastings that she had so far overcome her reluctance and disregarded
her nerves "as to unloose the Prince, so that wrapping-paper may no
longer bar his 'progress.'" For a detailed account of the "progress" of
the volume, see *Christina Rossetti*, pp. 202–207, and *Ross. Pprs.*, pp.
69, 73, 74, *et passim.*

35 ❖ *D. G. Rossetti to Alexander Macmillan*

26 Feb 1865
16 Cheyne Walk
Chelsea

My dear Macmillan

Many sincere thanks for the drawing, which I value highly (so highly that I am all the more sensible that it is more than I have really any business to accept) and for the photos, which are just as good as the drawing. I shall find some photos: of my own drawings, of which to beg your acceptance. The block is at last <u>finally</u> with the printer. But the proofs he has sent me hitherto are not successful. He is to send me another, I trust, tomorrow.

Ever yours
DG Rossetti

36 ❖ *W. M. Rossetti to Alexander Macmillan*

166 Albany St.
26 Feb. [1865]

Dear Macmillan,

Having now looked more minutely into the details, I find that it would be convenient to me to have 30 copies of the Dante here—some for bestowal, others for contingencies or stock. Would you send them up at your convenience.

Would you also please forward a copy of Christina's new edition, as soon as out to

The Rev^d. James Ford
Hirondelle
Torquay—

& put it down to my account. If a Dante addressed to the same gentleman has not yet gone off, the two might, at your pleasure, be forwarded together.

Yours truly,
W. M. Rossetti

81 High Street
Hastings
Tuesday morning [March, 1865]

My dear Mr. Macmillan

I don't know whom to bore, so I arbitrarily select you, count-
ing on your kindly excusing the trouble I give you.

Days ago I received and sent back to Mr. Masson a Mag.
proof, writing on its corner that I wanted a revise. This revise
has not reached me; and as I made two alterations of some
importance in the proof, I am naturally anxious to see the revise. Perhaps I was quite wrong in sending the proof at all to
Mr. Masson, but there was no printer's address on it.—The gist
of which long story is that if through your kind intervention
I can gain sight of my revise, I shall be duly obliged.

What has become of my 2nd Edition? William's *Dante* has
turned out comely and delightful. My Vol. 2 has got to Gabriel,
so I hope it will at any rate soon go on to you.[1]

Sincerely yours
Christina G. Rossetti

---

[1] In a letter to Dante Gabriel William dates March 3rd, under the
heading, *"Transmission to Mac,"* Christina wrote, "Might I, instead
of sending them direct, send them [the poems in vol. 2] through your
brotherly hands? When I have put them in order, I should be so
glad if you would put the finishing touch to their arrangement. That
is one reason for wishing to send them through you; and another is
that then I foresee you will charitably do the business-details; my wish
being for the same terms as *Goblin Market*. One single piece in Vol. 2
belongs neither to Mac nor to myself; to wit, *L.E.L.* [*Works*, p. 344];
but I have Miss Emily Faithfull's permission to make use of it. . . ."
Emily Faithfull (1835–1895) founded and edited *The Victoria Press*
(1863–1880). Christina contributed several poems to her relief publications in 1863, *A Royal Princess* to *Poems: An Offering to Lancashire*
edited by Isa Craig and *Dream Love* to *A Welcome*. *L.E.L.* may likewise
have been donated to a publication of this sort, in which the author
temporarily renounced copyright privileges.

In the same letter Christina requested her brother to go over her proofs as they were printed off. In which case, "you had better have them before they come to me: and then I think I shall send them home for lynx-eyed research after errors, before letting them go to press" (*Ross. Pprs.,* pp. 81–82). The four Rossettis made a practice of criticizing, editing, and proofreading one another's manuscripts in preparing them for publication. See above, Lttr. 29.

38 ❖ *Christina Rossetti to Alexander Macmillan*

81 High Street
Hastings
23rd [March, 1865]

My dear Mr. Macmillan

I won't be such a bore again about a Magazine proof; though long ago one came out unrectified, which alarmed me: but I dare say this one will appear quite right. Pray pardon me. I fancy one of the two pieces I received in proof <u>will</u> be in the April no., because it names April. Mr. Masson has one more thing of mine still in hand unprinted, should he judge it available:[1] I am very glad when he finds space for me. Thank you for making me so welcome.

I did not know my 2nd Edition was out. Will you oblige me by ordering a copy to be sent to

Mrs. Gemmer[2]
Care of Mrs. Bland
181 Albany Street N.W.:—

also by forwarding me *here* a copy of Mr. Allingham's *Ballad Book*. I hope I enclose the proper stamps.

That announcement in the *Athenæum*[3] did not take you by surprize, much more than a similar one in the *Morning Star* did me. How either got in I know not. But though they take your acceptance for granted (which I don't), they give my title correctly. I hope you will soon have my <u>Vol. 2</u> to judge of: it went to Gabriel some short while ago.

I am much stronger now, thank you, than when I came

here, and hope to be at home again in a week or a fortnight.

Yours very truly

Christina G. Rossetti [4]

---

[1] In December CGR had sent "three . . . pot-boilers to Mac's Mag." The two printed the following spring were *Spring Fancies* (April, 1865), p. 460, and *Last Night* (May, 1865), p. 48 (both in *Works,* p. 361).

[2] Caroline Gemmer also wrote under the name of Gerda Fay. Her published volumes include *Poetry for Play Hours* (1860), *Lyrics and Idylls* (1861), *Children of the Sun* (1869), *Babyland* . . . (1877), and *Poems, Westminster* (1897). An occasional caller at the Rossettis, she was one of the women "not without literary practice" whom Christina recommended to John H. Ingram for his *Eminent Women* series. See above, Lttr. 6, n. 1, and below, Lttrs. 71 and n. 2, 98.

[3] "Miss Christina Rossetti will soon publish by Messrs. Macmillan, another volume of poems, of about the same bulk as that entitled 'Goblin Market' by the same lady. Like the latter, the new book will be illustrated by two designs by Mr. D. G. Rossetti. The proposed title is 'The Prince's Progress, and Other Poems'" (*Ath.,* March 18, 1865, p. 387).

[4] Marginal note by the firm on top of the letter: "[7 sh.] in stamps returned."

39 ❖ *D. G. Rossetti to Alexander Macmillan*

March 27 [1865]
16 Cheyne Walk
Chelsea

My dear Macmillan

I will send on the M.S.S. to you in a day or two at furthest

Yours ever

DG Rossetti

40 ❖ *Christina Rossetti to Alexander Macmillan*

81 High Street
Hastings
Monday [March, 1865]

My dear Mr. Macmillan

The Ballad Book has come safely to hand, and very pretty its contents look.[1]

Thank you for your exposition of my unknown privileges, and for the misguided stamps. Will you, please, let me have one copy of my 2ⁿᵈ Edition here; I don't know that I shall want any more, at any rate I don't yet.

Yours very truly
Christina G. Rossetti

I see my *Prince's Progress* is announced also in the *Guardian*. How did it first get it?

---

[1] Marginal note on top (incomplete), presumably by Christina: ". . . don't pay postage for the Ballad Book: thanks."

41 ❖ *Christina Rossetti to Alexander Macmillan*

81 High Street
Hastings
30th [March, 1865]

My dear Mr. Macmillan

I shall be most especially pleased if you will begin on Vol. 2 when it gets to you; if, that is, you are not disappointed in it.[1] It seems not impossible, (though so pleasant as to suggest improbability) that by the end of May I may go with William to get my first glimpse of Italy: could it anyhow be managed that my proof labours should be over by then? in case of need.

Yours very truly
Christina G. Rossetti

---

[1] Marginal note by Christina on top: "I am so glad the binding pleased you better, of *Goblin Market*."

42 ❖ *D. G. Rossetti to Alexander Macmillan*

31 March 1865
16 Cheyne Walk
Chelsea

My dear Macmillan

You will get the MSS almost immediately, but I am await-
ing a reply from my sister to one or two points proposed to
her yesterday.[1] Will you send me a copy of Goblin Market
2nd Ed. I am anxious to see how the blocks are printed. I hear
you have not adopted the colour I chose from a set of specimens sent, for the binding, but another, which is all right if it
sells the book better. But I hope to find that there is a mistake
in a report I hear that my design for the binding has been
somehow clipped or altered. This should no more occur without my sanction than an alteration should be made in en-
graving my drawings.

Yours sincerely
DG Rossetti

[1] Actually Gabriel proposed major changes in some six poems. "After
six well-defined and several paroxysms of stamping, foaming, hair-
uprooting," CGR replied the same day, "it seems time to assume a
treacherous calm: and in this (comparatively) lucid interval I regain
speech." She discusses each of the changes in turn, and concludes,
"After all which, I shall hope the MS. WILL go to Mr. Macmillan; but,
if that enterprizing publisher has been prodding you, it is di proprio
moto, not instigated in word by me. Your woodcuts are so essential to
my contentment that I will wait a year for them if need is—though
(in a whisper) six months would better please me. But perhaps it might
be as well to commence printing as soon as may be, in case that Fata
Morgana of delight, my sight of Italy with William, should by any
manner of means come to pass; of course IF the proofs could be got
through before our start in May, it would be charming" (*Ross. Pprs.,*
pp. 94–95).

43 ❖ *D. G. Rossetti to Alexander Macmillan*

Text: Macmillan MS. Published: *N&Q* (March, 1962), pp. 97–98.

4 April 1865
16 Cheyne Walk
Chelsea

My dear Macmillan

With this I post to you (by book post) the M.S. of *The Prince's Progress and other poems.* Christina is anxious to get on with the printing immediately as it is not unlikely she may be going to Italy in May & would like to see all the proofs before then. I wish you'd always send <one> a proof to me at the same time as to her, & not print off till <u>both</u> are returned to you—I'll see to my 2 drawings as soon as possible.

Pray pardon my oblivious [*sic*] alarm about the binding. On seeing it I saw it was improved & even guessed I might have had a hand in it, though many things meanwhile had so put the matter out of my mind that I can't even recall it now. As for the colour it's "dreffle," but never mind.

By the bye you always reverse my signature in advertisements. Will you oblige me by henceforth printing it as when I am (& when am I not?)

Sincerely yours
<u>D. G.</u> Rossetti [1]
I   2

---

[1] In 1866 Gabriel made a similar request to his Aunt Charlotte Polidori (*DGRFL,* II, 187):

. . . By the bye, let me ask you a favour. Will you kindly address me as in the signature of this letter? I have so written my name nearly all my life, and variations in one's nomenclature are apt to create confusion. Not that the matter is of consequence to any one, not even greatly to

Your affectionate Nephew
D. G. Rossetti

44 ❖ *D. G. Rossetti to Alexander Macmillan*

26 April 1865
16 Cheyne Walk
Chelsea

My dear Macmillan,

I send sheet <u>E</u> this morning with the sheets of the *Prince's Progress*. It does not belong to that book but some other queer collection. Would you let me have by bearer the proper sheet unless you can send me (which I particularly wish) a complete set of the <u>revised</u> sheets (these sent are not so) as I want to see what corrections my sister has made in some instances. I dare say you could give the bearer such a set for me.

I am very sorry to be the cause of any delay with the book now, but fear it will be quite impossible for me to do the 2 blocks before some time towards the end of May. I am so full of other work that sooner seems impracticable. The sketch for the binding I'll look up & send you at once—

Ever yours
DG Rossetti

45 ❖ *D. G. Rossetti to Alexander Macmillan*

28 April 1865
16 Cheyne Walk
Chelsea

My dear Macmillan

I shall be glad to see your Cambridge friend (especially in your company) on Wednesday or Friday of next week, whichever day suits you best, at 11 A.M. Will you kindly let me know.

I enclose a sketch for the binding of *P.'s P.,* & shall be glad to choose the colour. I rather incline to white, only in such case the cloth must be strained on <u>whitened</u> boards. By this means I made Swinburne's book look really white.

I find on inquiry that my sister is very anxious not to dispense with the 2 drawings I promised her, so I think we must [then] wait till I can do them which shall be as soon as possible.

I asked her the other day what business arrangement she had made with you as to this new volume, & found that nothing had been said on the point. I therefore got her leave to say a word. Now couldn't you be a good fairy & give her something down for this edition,—say £100? You know she is a good poet, & some day people will know it. That's so true that it comes in rhyme of itself! She's going to Italy and would find a little moneybag useful.

Please let me have the revised sheets when you can & believe me

Ever yours
DG Rossetti

A. Macmillan Esq.

46 ❖ *Christina Rossetti to D. G. Rossetti*
Text: Troxell, pp. 146–147 (postscript omitted).

166 Albany Street
N.W.
Wednesday night [April–May, 1865] [1]

MY DEAR GABRIEL

I am truly sorry for annoyance brought on you by your brotherliness in helping me as to business matters. Mr. Macmillan writes under a complete misapprehension as to my Italian-tour-fund, precarious indeed if it depended on P. P. instead of on unfailing family bounty. However, now I will write direct to him and set matters as straight as words can set them: I am perfectly willing to let vol. 2 appear on the same terms as vol. 1., and very likely these terms are both what suit him best, and what in the long run will do at least as well for me as any others. So please wash your hands of the vexatious business; I will settle it now myself with him. What made him combine my Italian holiday with the proceeds of vol. 2. I know not: it may have been a guess founded on (apparent) probability, or he may have supposed that my motive in wishing to get through the proofs before setting off was to bag the money,—of course it <u>was</u> merely not to delay the publication.

Mama's love.
Your obliged affect. sister
Christina G. Rossetti

---

[1] The square brackets are mine. I date this letter according to internal evidence. See above, Lttr. 45.

47 ❖ W. M. Rossetti to Alexander Macmillan

166 Albany St. N. W.
30 April [1865]

Dear Macmillan,

Could you give me any idea of how—or I say "whether at all"?—the Dante is selling. Some few weeks ago a friend told me that he had asked about the book at Willis & Sotheran's, & they informed him that they had taken 3 dozen copies, & had disposed of them all—which rather & agreeably surprised me. If anything not wholly unfavourable can be said about it, I should now begin to think about continuing the translation—[1] of which I might perhaps do a little during a visit to Italy with my Mother & Christina which I project starting upon before May is out.[2]

Yours truly,
W. M. Rossetti

Thanks for the Nonconformist you sent me.

How about advertizing? I suppose some little should be done in that line just at the Dante Festival time, about 24 May: my <u>wish</u> however is to economize in that direction as far as reasonable & not self-harming.

---

[1] William translated nineteen cantos of the *Purgatorio,* then dropped

the matter until 1900 when he attempted unsuccessfully to get them published. The *Inferno* received fairly favorable reviews. The reviewer for *The Athenæum,* which gave the work considerable attention, called it "an elegant little volume," but took William to task for the literalness of his translation (April 1, 1865), p. 453. Several issues later William defended his work in a letter to the editor, which was followed by the reviewer's reply.

² William, Christina, and Mrs. Rossetti left for the Continent May 22, went to Italy by way of France and Switzerland, spent June traveling in Italy, and returned to London June 26 (*Ross. Pprs.,* pp. 104–131). See below, Lttr. 48 and *Christina Rossetti,* pp. 209–211.

48 ⋄ *W. M. Rossetti to Alexander Macmillan*

Inland Revenue Office,
Somerset House
10 July [1865]

Dear Macmillan,

On returning from abroad, I find that you were so good as to send £1 (or £1.1., I forget which) in payment for a few verses of mine on Lincoln in your magazine, & that my sister, not knowing the facts, returned the money. This is simply to say that, whenever it suits you to send the money back, it will find its rightful home in my pocket.

My mother & Christina, with myself, got to Milan & Verona & a few intermediate Italian towns, going by the St. Gothard route, & returning by the Iflugen: it was a great delight to us all. As to its effect on Christina's health, I am sorry to say it did not produce the sensible improvement I had hoped for; her strength, power of continuous exertion, etc., not appearing to be decidedly greater at the end of the trip than at the beginning. However, she got on fairly on the whole, & since her return, barring the first few days, she seems very tolerable.

Yours truly,
W. M. Rossetti

Text: Macmillan MS. *Extract published, N&Q* (March, 1962), p. 98.

3 Dec 1865
16 Cheyne Walk
Chelsea

My dear Macmillan

I dare say you have been giving me over to a reprobate mind
—but I'm really about the 2 drawings for my sister's book now
& hope yet to send them you before very many days.

Linton [1] I find is in Cumberland. I should rather like to send
them to him to be cut, but if there is not time for this will try
Swain I think.

I've got to get the binder to make some slight changes in the
cover. That is, all the lines must be made half their present
thickness (from the outside in each instance) and the gold
balls turned into rings—the colour I chose is a green one which
I have by me.

I hope all is well with you and yours. I am
ever yours sincerely
DG Rossetti   turn over [DGR]

P.S. There are still by some misadventure several faults of
print in the volume. One occurring at page 70 in a very beautiful poem is well worth a cancel in my opinion.[2]

—— hid her coil.
Where grass grew thickest,
bird and beast etc.

should say

—— hid her coil
Where grass grew thickest.
Bird and beast etc.

I am writing to my sister about it.

---

[1] William James Linton (1812–1898), wood-engraver and poet. He
illustrated Gilchrist's *Blake* and engraved Gabriel's designs for *Prince's*

Progress. The two men first met when Gabriel was designing the woodcuts for Moxon's illustrated *Tennyson* (1857). He thought Linton "a most agreeable fellow" and by far "the best engraver living." Dissatisfied with the work of the Dalziel brothers, he withdrew several of the Tennyson designs from them and sent them to Linton instead. His opinion of the Dalziel brothers appears in the following lines he sent to W. B. Scott:

> O woodman, spare that block,
> O gash not anyhow;
> It took ten days by clock,
> I'd fain protect it now.
> Chorus, wild laughter from Dalziel's workshop.

[2] I have treated the extremely complicated textual history of this misprint in my article, "Christina Rossetti's *Songs in a Cornfield:* A Misprint Uncorrected," *N&Q* (March, 1962), pp. 97–100. After a number of alterations the final variant as printed in the *Works* (pp. 369–371) reads:

> A silence of full noontide heat
> Grew on them at their toil;
> The farmer's dog woke up from sleep,
> The green snake hid her coil
> Where grass stood thickest; bird and beast
> Sought shadows as they could,
> The reaping men and women paused
> And sat down where they stood;
> They ate and drank and were refreshed,
> For rest from toil is good.

50 ❖ *Christina Rossetti to Alexander Macmillan*
Text: Macmillan MS. *Extract published, N&Q* (March, 1962), p. 98.

166 Albany St. N.W.
5th December 1865.

My dear Mr. Macmillan

Now that my vol. seems really on the eve of coming out Gabriel urges me to ask for an <u>Errata</u> (needful, alas!), and for two <u>Cancels</u>. Let me join my request to his, as the cases are important—one or two of them I do suspect must have got wrong after my final revision.[1] Please oblige me so far.

Your Mag. has so long had a little thing [2] of mine lying by, that I <suppose> conjecture the Editor may justly judge it unfit for publication. If so I hope to see it back in my own hands some day.

Very truly yours
Christina G. Rossetti

---

[1] See above, Lttr. 49, n. 2.

[2] I do not identify the piece. However, in 1866 the magazine printed four of CGR's poems: *Consider* (Jan.), p. 232 (*Works*, p. 237), *Helen Grey* (March), p. 375 (*Works*, p. 355), *By the Waters of Babylon* (Oct.), pp. 424–426 (*Works*, p. 239), and *Seasons* (Dec.), pp. 168–169 (*Works*, p. 309).

51 ❖ *Christina Rossetti to Alexander Macmillan*
Text: Macmillan MS. *Extract published, N&Q* (March, 1962), pp. 98–99.

166 Albany St. N.W.
16th December [1865]

Dear Mr. Macmillan

First for something not unpleasant: I think the hand-corrections will do beautifully, and beg you to oblige me by having them executed. Secondly for the old sore: you know the woodcuts cannot be ready for Xmas?—I hardly know how to ask you now to keep back *P. P.* after your "few days" advertisement;—yet if you agree with me in thinking Gabriel's designs too desirable to forego, I will try to follow your example of patience under disappointment.

I received a kind letter from Mr. Masson about the *Magazine:* thank you.

Yours very sincerely
Christina G. Rossetti

1866–1869

The 1866 letters continue with the production details concerned with the publication of *Prince's Progress*, which appeared in June. Several letters request Macmillan's consideration of work submitted by friends of the Rossettis. Christina writes about her poems published in the Magazine. William writes about his *Fine Art, chiefly Contemporary*, which Macmillan published in 1867.

52 ❖ *Christina Rossetti to Alexander Macmillan*

166 Albany St. N.W.
3rd January 1866

Dear Mr. Macmillan

All best new year's wishes to you and yours. But of course this is a business letter. May I trouble you to read the note which I enclose, and to oblige me by ordering a copy of *Goblin Market* to be forwarded to the address Mr. Niles [1] gives in his P.S. I do not know whether you may think it well to let a copy of *Pr. Pr.* accompany *G. M.;* you approving, I should be well inclined to let him have it at once; but of course the interests of our English edition must be first of all considered. Meanwhile I enclose stamps.

Yours very truly
Christina G. Rossetti

---

[1] See below, Lttr. 53, n. 2.

53 ❖ *Christina Rossetti to* [*Thomas Niles*] [1]
Text: Troxell, pp. 153–154.

3rd January 1866

SIR

Through the kindness of Miss Ingelow I have been favoured with your letter of the 29th.

Allow me through you to thank Mess[rs]. Roberts Brothers

for their liberal proposal:[2] I am well aware that I can put in no claim to any such arrangement; but shall gladly accept your offer, having had no dealings on the subject with any other American publisher. I will therefore direct that a copy of *Goblin Market* be forwarded to your London address: and perhaps I had better mention that the whole volume belongs to me with the exception of 5 pieces (*Round Tower at Jhansi— Maude Clare—Uphill—Birthday—Apple-gathering*) which are the property of two publishers.[3] If I can manage it my forth-coming volume shall accompany *Goblin Market;* but I am not sure whether it can be sent you quite yet, as of course I must consult Mr. Macmillan, to whom indeed a portion of the copyright belongs.

> Pray, Sir, believe me
> Sincerely yours
> Christina G. Rossetti

---

[1] Square brackets mine.

[2] The firm of Roberts Brothers of Boston (taken over by Little, Brown, & Co., 1898) was started by Lewis A. Roberts (b. 1833), book-binder and manufacturer of photograph albums. It was not until his brother-in-law, Thomas Niles (b. 1825) entered the business, first as an associate, then as a partner (1872), that the firm began its publishing career. The foundation of the firm's success was laid in 1863 when Niles first discovered and published Jean Ingelow's poetry in America; and as we see from Christina's letter, she was introduced to the firm by Miss Ingelow. Roberts Brothers became Gabriel's as well as Christina's American publisher, bringing out his *Poems* in 1870 and 1881. For further information about the history of the firm, see Madeleine B. Stern, *More Books, The Bulletin of the Boston Public Library,* Boston (December 1945), XX, No. 10, 419–424.

[3] The poems may be found in *Works,* pp. 332, 337, 339, 335. *Maude Clare* was published in *Once a Week* (Nov. 5, 1859), pp. 381–382. *Up-hill, A Birthday,* and *An Apple-Gathering* all appeared in *Macmillan's Magazine* in 1861 (Feb.), p. 325, (April), p. 498, (Aug.), p. 329 (see above, Introduction, p. 6). I do not know where the *Round Tower* first appeared or to which publisher it belonged, probably Macmillan.

My dear Mr. Masson

Bored as you are with contributions, many of them doubtless being poems good or bad by unknown authors, I feel ashamed to add the enclosed to the heap: the more so as personal acquaintanceship might make it more unpleasant for you to decline them. Will you therefore give me credit for sincerity when I beg you to accept all or any of the enclosed for *Macmillan's Magazine* in case you think them of any use, and to pass upon them a condign sentence of rejection in the (highly probable) opposite case.[1]

With William's and my own kindest regards to all at home, believe me

Truly yours

Christina G. Rossetti

45 Upper Albany St. N.W.

19th January [? 1866]

---

[1] Despite a discrepancy in dates, I place the letter here in the series on the assumption that Christina was sending Masson Isa Craig's poems. During the 1860's Christina seems to have interested herself in the literary fortunes of Isa Craig (1831–1903), a poetess and editor well known in her own day, now forgotten. In a letter William dates January, 1866, Gabriel refused his sister's request to illustrate Miss Craig's poems, sending her instead to Sandys or Hughes (*DGRFL*, II, 183–184). In October of the same year he himself applied to Miss Craig, then (?) the editor of *Argosy*, for illustrating work in behalf of C. F. Murray, whom he described as an extremely promising young artist (Univ. Texas MSS). Considering the fact that in the winter of 1866 *Argosy* (owned and later edited by Mrs. Henry Wood) published three of Christina's productions, one suspects that she may have been returning editorial favors. Her prose fiction piece, "Hero: a Metamorphosis," appeared in January, her poems, *Who Shall Deliver Me?* (*Works*, p. 238) in February and *If* (*Hoping Against Hope, Works*, p. 365) in March.

However, the obligation may well have been on Miss Craig's instead of Christina's side. It will be recalled that in 1863 Christina donated a poem to Miss Craig's edition of the anthology published for the benefit of the relief fund for the Lancashire cotton hands (see above, Lttr. 37, n. 1), to which Dante Gabriel also contributed his sonnet, *Sudden Light*. The Upper Albany address likewise leads me to believe that the letter dates earlier than 1866, possibly 1864. It could not have been written later than 1867, for that year the Rossettis moved to Euston Square and Masson was succeeded by George Grove as editor of *Macmillan's* (see above, Lttr. 29, n. 1, and below, Lttr. 86, n. 4).

55 ❖ *D. G. Rossetti to Alexander Macmillan*

Tuesday   30 January 1866
16 Cheyne Walk
Chelsea

My dear Macmillan,
One block will lacking go to Linton (who I think will be the best man) on Thursday or Friday.

I do not myself see what the American publishers can want with the woodcuts which they will not of course reproduce— The other shall follow without delay.

Ever yours
DG Rossetti

56 ❖ *D. G. Rossetti to Alexander Macmillan*

29 March
1866
16 Cheyne Walk
Chelsea

My dear Macmillan
As it is not yet the First of April, will you believe me when I say that the block is done & gone to Linton, who has my request to be as expeditious as may be—

Now then is the time for the binder to correct the binding— I send <you one> him with this a cover representing the colour which I wish adopted among those I received, and the necessary alterations. I write you word of my doing so that you may keep him to time—

Ever yours
DG Rossetti

57 ❖ *D. G. Rossetti to Alexander Macmillan*

5 April/66
16 Cheyne Walk
Chelsea

My dear Macmillan
A friend of mine, Mr. Smetham[1] the artist, has been asked to review Blake's Life for the London (Quarterly) Review, but has not the book. As he is a highly desirable reviewer, I said I had no doubt you would send him a copy. His address is

Jas. Smetham Esq
1 Park Lane
Paradise Row
Stoke Newington

I have not yet got a proof of the block from Linton but expect one before long.

Ever yours
DG Rossetti

---

[1] James Smetham (1821–1889), a painter of religious subjects, was a valued member of the Rossetti circle from the time Dante Gabriel first met him at Cary's Academy in 1843. In the course of their friendship Dante Gabriel "promoted, so far as he could, the sale of his pictures" (*Remin.*, II, 323–324). See below, Lttr. 94.

58 ❖ *D. G. Rossetti to Alexander Macmillan*
Text: Macmillan MS. Published: *N&Q* (March, 1962), p. 99.

21 April [1866]
16 Cheyne Walk

My dear Macmillan
Will you kindly give orders, now the cuts <u>are</u> done, that

thorough care should be taken with the printing. Let me see a proof. The Goblin Market was so ill done in this respect as to be a fresh annoyance every time I see a copy. Linton has taken great pains—the large block especially giving him I am sure a great deal of trouble—and I would like his name to appear on the title-page (if not already reprinted) thus:

With 2 designs by D G Rossetti
engraved by W. J. Linton

The bookbinder has sent me a cover which is now quite right —the green of this cover is the one to be adopted for the edition.

Ever yours
DG Rossetti

59 ❖ D. G. Rossetti to Alexander Macmillan

16 Cheyne Walk
24 July 1866

My dear Macmillan

I am sending you by book post a pen & ink drawing which my sister has received through a friend. It illustrates one of her poems, and is the work of a young artist named Rivington,[1] unknown to her and to me, who greatly desires to illustrate an edition or selection of her poems, if any such thing were in contemplation or could be entertained. My own opinion of the design is that it shows very high poetic feeling, and is in a most remarkable degree in sympathy with my sister's work. In certain technical respects it shows a little immaturity, but as I see it is dated 2 years back and hear that the artist has since been studying hard, I have no doubt he is making great advances in knowledge & practice. It is no exaggeration to say that this design of his proves him to have natural gifts of the highest order. You will be the best judge whether any such project is feasible, but I am instructed (by his friend through whom the drawing . . . [remainder missing].

---

[1] William notes in his diary for July 12, 1867 that "Dodgson (the Oxford man and photographer) writes to Christina to say that a friend

of his, Rivington, would much like to illustrate either of Christina's volumes and would do it at little cost. D sends a design by R from *Passing Away* [*Works*, p. 190]; which, though not advanced in execution is finely felt, and a good deal like what C herself might do if she knew enough to draw . . ." (*Ross. Pprs.*, p. 236). Like Dodgson (Lewis Carroll), J. A. Rivington was a clergyman. There seems to be some discrepancy in dates, for DGR's letter is clearly dated July 24, 1866. In 1879 he sent Christina what was apparently the same pen-and-ink design to the poem, with the date 1865 in the corner. "I am enclosing a production which I think I once mentioned to you and you did not seem to remember," he explained; "but I fancy you did see it when sent to me by some one long ago as the work of a young amateur or artist whose name I know not. It is certainly poetic and assuredly quaint enough. Now you have it, keep it if you care. I turned it up yesterday, and bethought me to send it ere it got buried again in heaps." William identifies the design and its date, and the artist (*Fam. Lttrs.*, p. 78).

60 ❖ *Christina Rossetti to Alexander Macmillan*

166 Albany St. N.W.
Friday morning [December, 1866] [1]

Dear Mr. Macmillan

Will you and yours accept my best Xmas and New Year's wishes, and my sympathy in the sorrow that has sobered your joys. Happily the great joy of Xmas can light up any sorrow.

I enclose my receipt with thanks; and won't forget your suggestion to send direct to you for the Magazine.

Always yours truly
Christina G. Rossetti

---

[1] I date this letter according to internal evidence. The month is obviously December, the year probably 1866, for the Rossettis moved away from Albany Street in the summer of 1867 and Christina was in Hastings in December, 1865. In June of 1866 Macmillan lost his youngest son Willie, to whose life he had "looked forward . . . with peculiar hope," and who was "the light and joy of our house" (*Macm. Lttrs.*, Glasgow ed., pp. xli, 211).

61 ❖ W. M. Rossetti to Alexander Macmillan

166 Albany St. N.W.

7 June. [1867] [1]

Dear Macmillan,

At the last (& I fear too late) moment I noticed a stupid misprint in my book; [2] & if possible would like to insert an Errata for this & one other less important mistake. To save time I address you rather than the printer. Don't trouble yourself to answer this.

Yours very truly,

W. M. Rossetti

---

[1] I date this letter and those following (62–66) according to the year date written in by Macmillan or a member of the firm.

[2] *Fine Art, chiefly Contemporary,* published by Macmillan in 1867. This was a collection of essays and articles about living artists, previously published in various periodicals.

62 ❖ W. M. Rossetti to Alexander Macmillan

166 Albany St. N.W.

10 June. [1867]

Dear Macmillan,

A letter of yours to Christina apprises me that my book is now published. I have not yet received a copy; & wd. therefore be obliged to you if you wd. let me have 2 at this house at your earliest convenience.

Also wd. you send out copies to the persons on the enclosed list. I really don't know whether any or how many copies are considered to be properly mine by right or accustomed courtesy: so please to hold me your debtor for any of these copies to wh. I am not reasonably entitled. I <u>must</u> either way bestow these copies gratis—chiefly on the ground that the recipients have already bestowed gratis on me copies of books by them. This list includes all the absolutely necessary names I remember at present; but perhaps one or two more may strike my recollection afterwards. I say nothing about copies for reviews, as no doubt you will do what you consider requisite in that direction.

Yours always truly

W. M. Rossetti

I don't yet know for certain whether the book will actually appear in an American edition. Mr. Niles was out of town when I called to speak to him, but we have interchanged letters on the subject.

62A ENCLOSURE,[1] *W. M. Rossetti*
to Alexander Macmillan

1   D. G. Rossetti, 16 Cheyne Walk, S.W.
2   Miss Madox Brown, 37 Fitzroy Sq. W.
3   Miss Howell, 3 York Villas, Brixton, S.W.
4   F. G. Stephens, 10 Hammersmith Terr. W.
5   F. T. Palgrave, 5 York Pl., Regents' Park N.W.
6   A. C. Swinburne, 22a Dorset St., Portman Sq. W.
7   W. B. Scott, 33 Elgin Road, Kensington Park W.
8   Wm. Morris, 26 Queen Sq. W.C.
9   Thos Woolner, 29 Welbeck St. W.
10   C. B. Cayley, 5 Montpelier Row, Blackheath [W.C.]

---

[1] Most of the persons on William's list are too well known to need identification. Miss Madox Brown was Lucy, Ford Madox Brown's daughter and the future Mrs. William Rossetti. F. G. Stephens, the art critic, and Thomas Woolner, the sculptor, were original members of the Pre-Raphaelite Brotherhood. Miss Kate (Frances Catherine) Howell was the cousin, later the wife, of Charles Augustus Howell, colorful Anglo-Portuguese adventurer, DGR's art agent and friend, who undertook the exhumation for him in 1869. Howell married his cousin Kate (often called Kitty) August 21, 1867. See Christina's unpublished letters to the Howells (Univ. Texas MSS). For an interesting and informative biography of Howell, consult Helen Rossetti Angeli, *Pre-Raphaelite Twilight* (1954). Charles Bagot Cayley (1823–1883) was in love with Christina. He proposed to her in 1866 and was refused. Further details may be found in my *Christina Rossetti*.

63 ❖ W. M. Rossetti to Alexander Macmillan

166 Albany St. N.W.

11 June [1867]

Dear Macmillan,

Thanks for the copies received early this afternoon. The book looks a very creditable one to your firm so far as its outer man is concerned. I hope its inner man may be found proportional.

You seem to have sent the book to a very fair number of papers. The only other papers—wh. however I must leave entirely to your decision—that occur to my mind are the following—

1 The London Review.[1] I scarcely know whether it is now of sufficient importance. It was very civil to my Swinburne volume, & has been drawn upon in the present reissue.

2 The Chronicle[2] (24 Tavistock St.). This is the only paper I am now writing in. So far as I have observed, it gets from circulating libraries all the books it reviews; & I don't know whether or not its policy wd. be to notice a contributor, even were his work forwarded. It is a very creditable paper, newly started. I cannot vouch for its circulation.

3 Edinburgh Courant. There have been, & as far as I know still are, two leading writers[3] on this paper friends of mine, & previous publications in our family have been well received in the Courant.

4 Fraser. This is freely drawn on in the reissue,[4] & I think it more likely than not that the book wd. receive a review. Can't say however—nor do I know whether there is any occasion to send it.

5 Westminster Review. I know the gentleman who does a large proportion of the quarterly notice of books, & have little doubt he wd. mention the book if it comes before him: maybe this will be equally the case whether or not the book is sent.[5]

With thanks for all your attention to this venture

Yours always truly,

W. M. Rossetti

I think I ought to send a copy to
Wm. Allingham
Lymington, Hants.
Please debit me accordingly.[6]

---

[1] The *London Review* was started by Charles Mackay in 1860. A competitor of the influential *Saturday Review*, "it came nearest to being a success when a part of its staff consisted of men temporarily estranged from the *Saturday*" (M. M. Bevington, *The Saturday Review 1855–1868*, New York, 1941, p. 320 and n.). Toward 1862 WMR was art critic for the journal, then under the editorship of Patrick Comyn. William's *Swinburne's Poems and Ballads; a Criticism* was published by Hotten in 1866.

[2] A paper not to be confused with the *Morning Chronicle*. Started in March, 1867, under the editorship of a Mr. Wetherall, the weekly, designed as a liberal Catholic organ, lasted barely a year. In 1867 William wrote for it his highly favorable criticism of Walt Whitman's *Leaves of Grass,* described by John Burroughs, U.S. Comptroller of the Currency, as "a grand and lofty piece of criticism," which "has had its effect here."

[3] One was James Hannay (see above, Lttr. 18 and n. 2). The other may have been P. P. Alexander or W. B. Scott. I do not identify the previous publication by the Rossettis. Possibly William was referring to a review of the Gilchrist *Blake* by Hannay.

[4] Between 1861 and 1864 WMR wrote reviews of art exhibits for *Fraser's,* edited by J. A. Froude from 1860 to 1874. *Fine Art* was not reviewed, however.

[5] A favorable review appeared in *Westminster* (Oct. 1, 1867), pp. 605–606. Although the writer thought William too biased and too subjective to be "quite a reliable critic," he granted that "no such valuable essays have appeared since Mr. Palgrave's criticism on Art," and recommended to "those who would truly understand Millais, Holman Hunt, and Leighton," that they "study Mr. Rossetti's page, and learn to see their works in the same spirit in which he sees them." I do not know who wrote the review.

[6] Marginal note by the firm on the bottom of the page confirms the year date: "Post June 22, 1867."

64 ❖ *Christina Rossetti to The Firm*

56 Euston Square, N.W.
Saturday evening. [July 1. 1867] [1]

Miss C. Rossetti begs that a copy of "Prince's Progress" may be sent to

Mrs. Boldemann [2]
34 Marlborough Hill
S. John's Wood
N.W.—

and encloses stamps for postage;—and calls attention to her change of address.[3]

---

[1] I date the letter July because of a marginal note at the bottom which reads, "Sent July 1st. 1867," but it may well have been written toward the end of June.

[2] I do not identify her.

[3] See Lttr. 60 and n. 1. The Rossettis lived at 166 Albany Street from 1854 to 1867 and at 56 Euston Square until 1876, at which time owing to family disagreements, CGR and her mother took up their residence at 30 Torrington Square and William and Lucy, married in 1874, remained at Euston Square (see below, Lttr. 114, n. 1). Maria Rossetti left to join an Anglican Sisterhood (see below, Lttr. 95, n. 2).

65 ❖ *Christina Rossetti to Alexander Macmillan*

56 Euston Square, N.W. [Spring, 1868]

Dear Mr. Macmillan

Thank you for such a handsome sum. It is honorably formidable to appear in one no. with Tennyson.[1] How pretty your grounds must be looking now in the spring: I hope to see something pretty too next week as my Mother and I shall be going to Gloucester.[2]

Very truly yours
Christina G. Rossetti

---

[1] Probably in payment for CGR's long poem *Mother Country* (*Works,* p. 245), published in the *Magazine* March, 1868, p. 403. Two of her

poems appeared in the May issue (p. 86) which featured Tennyson's *Lucretius*. They were *A Smile and a Sigh* (*Works,* p. 380) and *Dead Hope* (*Works,* p. 377).

[2] To visit CGR's maternal uncle, Henry Polydore (he Anglicized the Italian family name of Polidori), who lived in Gloucester and practiced law at Cheltenham.

66 ⬦ *Christina Rossetti to Alexander Macmillan*

56 Euston Square, N.W.
Thursday morning. [Autumn, 1868]

Dear Mr. Macmillan

Thank you again, and here is my full receipt.

Please remember me cordially to Mrs. Macmillan. I do keep up my invalid habits,[1] and certainly the winter is coming, but if some afternoon I find myself at the Elms [2] it will be pleasant.

Very truly yours
Christina G. Rossetti

---

[1] The preceding February (1867) William wrote in his diary that Christina had consulted the family physician Dr. Jenner (later Sir William Jenner, pioneer of vaccination in England), who told her she had "congestion of one lung, but certainly not consumption, that her life may be prolonged indefinitely, but she must not relax the precautions she has been taking of late years . . ." (*Ross. Pprs.,* p. 298). She died of cancer in 1894.

[2] Macmillan's residence at Upper Tooting from 1863 to 1884. Later what George Macmillan has called "the old-fashioned and commodious house" was re-christened Knapdale, after the region in Argyllshire where the Macmillan clan had originated.

67 ⬦ *W. M. Rossetti to Alexander Macmillan*

56 Euston Squ. N.W.
5 Sept. 1869.

Dear Macmillan,

This note will reach you thro' Mr. Keningale R. Cook,[1] a

gentleman whose acquaintance I have lately had the pleasure of making, & who has a volume of original poems he wishes to publish. I have looked thro' the poems to a certain extent, & have no hesitation in giving it as my opinion that the volume, when published, will not tarry long in giving Mr. Cook a certain recognized position among poetical writers.

As you are the publisher to whom he is minded to apply in the first instance, I have volunteered to give Mr. Cook these few lines of introductory message.

Believe me

Always truly yours

W. M. Rossetti

Alex. Macmillan Esq.

---

[1] An Italian connection of the Rossettis gave Cook a letter of introduction to William, who noted in his diary that his young caller had asked his advice about finding a publisher for his poetry. "He is a prepossessing young man, and evidently a man of intelligence. . . ." William observed (*Ross. Pprs.,* p. 406). At one time Cook was the editor of *The University Magazine,* a short-lived periodical (1877–1878), formerly *The Dublin University Magazine* (1844–1877). William, who had been contributing Shelley articles to it, arranged to introduce his sister into the magazine in 1877. Later she withdrew because of the "anti-Christian views" expressed in the magazine (Troxell, pp. 159–160).

1870–1871

In the spring of 1870 Christina changed publishers, an unfortunate move in her career. F. S. Ellis published her collection of prose tales *Commonplace* (1870), and Routledge her book of nursery rhymes *Sing-Song* (1872). She did not return to Macmillan until 1874. She was evidently acting under the influence of Dante Gabriel, who hoped to "concentrate our forces" by gathering together under Ellis's publishing banner "a little knot of congenial writers," that is, a literary coterie of producing poets consisting of himself, Christina, Swinburne, Morris, and W. B. Scott. Gabriel wrote Swinburne that his sister intended to leave Macmillan because Ellis would "pay much better—indeed I believe as well as can be managed." Although William agreed that Macmillan's terms were "obviously meagre," he was reluctant to have Christina sever connections with the firm. In fact her two brothers were working at cross purposes, for while William was trying to get better terms from Macmillan, both for *Sing-Song* and a collected edition of her poetry, Gabriel was trying to wean her away from "the staunch Mac."

Finally she put an end to her role as buffer between her two well-intentioned brothers and signed a contract with Ellis, who published her *Commonplace* at the same time as Gabriel's first volume, consisting principally of the poems he had buried in his wife's grave and then disinterred in the fall of 1869. The dismal failure of *Commonplace* compared to the brilliant and spectacular success of Gabriel's 1870 *Poems* was a discouraging experience for Christina, who thereupon voluntarily released Ellis from his obligation to publish *Sing-Song*. As a result, for two years she was left without a publisher. These were the years she was afflicted with Graves' disease, and was herself near death at a time (June, 1872) when Gabriel, brooding neurotically over Robert Buchanan's anonymous attacks (the first in the *Contemporary Review*, the second in an enlarged pamphlet), attempted suicide by taking laudanum.

The greater number of the letters in this group are from Christina to Ellis, and cover the critical period February–June, 1870. I include them in the present volume not only for their value as literary documents of great interest (particularly if they are compared to Oswald Doughty's edition of the *Letters of Dante Gabriel Rossetti to His Publisher, F. S. Ellis* [1928]), but also for the many references they contain to Macmillan and to unfinished business with the firm. Without these letters, Christina's publishing history would be incomplete and, consequently, the resumption of her business relations with Macmillan in 1874 would be less comprehensible.

As a group they are unpublished though I have drawn upon them freely for various published articles. They belong to the same British Museum collection (Additional MS 41, 130) that Professor Doughty used for his edition of Gabriel's letters to Ellis. With six exceptions Letters 68–87 are addressed to Ellis. The exceptions are two letters, one from Christina to Gabriel (73) and one from Gabriel to Christina (75), two letters from Ellis to Alice Boyd (82, 83), and two letters addressed to Macmillan (77, 86).

68 ❖ *Christina Rossetti to F. S. Ellis*

Text: British Museum MS [1]

56 Euston Square, N.W.
23rd February 1870.

SIR

I understand from my brother Mr. Rossetti that you are desirous of seeing some Nursery Rhymes I have just completed, and which I send you by book post. I shall be very glad if we can come to terms for their publication. I fear you may have misconceived what the illustrations amount to, as they are merely my own scratches and I cannot draw: [2] but I send you the M.S. just as it stands.

As regards the complete edition of my former vols., this cannot be gone into until the matter has been discussed with Mr. Macmillan, in whose hands is a large remainder of the 2nd ed. of Goblin Market. But my brother promises me to call on Mr. Macmillan and see what can be done some day.

The terms you named to Mr. Rossetti (¼ price of edition) I shall be very glad to accept, if you continue in the same mind.

Begging the favour of an early reply, I remain
Faithfully yours
Christina G. Rossetti

F. S. Ellis, Esq.

---

[1] The group of Christina's letters to Ellis in the British Museum collection consists of sixteen letters, one not addressed to Ellis (see below, Lttr. 149, n. 1). Fourteen belong to the 1870–1871 period; the fifteenth was written at a later date (see below, Lttr. 145). Since the series does

not in every instance follow the logical sequence of events, I have found it necessary to rearrange the group in chronological order.

² The original manuscript illustrated by Christina's "scratches" is still extant (Brit. Mus. MS Ash 1371).

69 ❖ *Christina Rossetti to F. S. Ellis*

Text: British Museum MS.

56 Euston Square, N.W.
25th February 1870

SIR

Very gladly I accept your terms, i.e., the fourth part of the publishing price of 500 copies of the *Nursery Rhymes* when they are ready for publication, it being understood that they are to be ready at a time I would beg you to define; and of 500 more when the first 500 are sold, and so on as each 500 is sold. By which however I beg not to bind myself never at any future time to publish them otherwise, though of course I have not the slightest present idea of so doing. Mr. Murray [1] is everything I can wish, if he can be induced to accept the commission; and if my scratches help to explain my meaning, so much the better. I hope for both our sakes the Rhymes may achieve some success, and remain

Faithfully yours
Christina G. Rossetti

---

[1] William writes that "Mr. Charles Fairfax Murray, the painter and art-expert, now owner of a very large and fine collection of works amid which those of Dante Rossetti figure conspicuously, became known to us as hardly more than a lad towards 1867, after he had first brought himself under the notice of Ruskin. Mr. Murray was always ready to do any friendly and good-natured service to my brother—such as copying his poems from the original manuscript, or sending him photographs . . . from Italian works of art interesting or useful to him" (*Remin.,* II, 325–26). Part of the Fairfax Murray collection was sold at Sotheby's, May 30, 1961, and is now the property of the University of Texas.

70 ❖ *Christina Rossetti to F. S. Ellis*

Text: British Museum MS. Published: *WHR* (Summer, 1962), p. 246.

56 Euston Square, N.W.
Monday evening, 28/2/70

Dear Sir

My brother is now engaged in attempting to arrange matters as to the large remainder of 'Goblin Market' with Mr. Macmillan,[1] and as I cannot foresee the result I let you know this, lest, pending such an arrangement, you should see fit to take no further steps as to 'SingSong.'[2] I for my part should be very glad at once to carry out our terms as stated in my letter of the 25th. Pray favour me with a reply and believe me

Truly yours,
Christina Georgina Rossetti

---

[1] The same day William wrote in his diary that he "called on Macmillan to talk over Christina's position with regard to him. . . . It is pretty clear that he would be ready to raise his offers heretofore made to C" (*Ross. Pprs.,* p. 499). Gabriel also wrote Allingham that "Christina has done a book of Nursery Rhymes, and is publishing with Ellis, who offers her much better terms than Mac does. She will leave Mac altogether" (*Lttrs. to Allingham,* p. 289).

[2] Christina's spelling of the title was often inconsistent.

71 ❖ *Christina Rossetti to F. S. Ellis*

Text: British Museum MS. *Extract published, WHR* (Summer, 1962), p. 246.

56 Euston Square, N.W.
3rd March 1870

Dear Sir

I most gladly close with the terms settled between us, and prefer waiting till publication to having any sum in advance. As for fixing a time for the book to come out, I only meant to fix such a time as shall ensure the business not dragging on indefinitely: suppose we say that the agreement between us lapses if 'SingSong' is not published by 1st July 1871? I will conclude that you assent to this unless I hear from you to the contrary. Your plan for illustrating 'Sing Song' pleases me, and I do indeed see the call for added bulk. You will [I] trust oblige me in due course by letting me correct the proofs.

I am now waiting for Macmillan's answer, my brother having twice called on him about my former volumes; and when I myself know I will also let you know.[1]

May I ask you a question, not for myself? A friend[2] of mine wishes to know what would be the cost of printing and publishing a very small collection of poems, say from 70 to 100 pages: can you tell me for her?

Faithfully yours,

Christina G. Rossetti

---

[1] Extract from William's diary: "Wednesday, 2 March.—Presented Macmillan with a comparative statement of the offers made to Christina by himself and Ellis . . ." (*Ross. Pprs.*, p. 499).

[2] I identify the "friend" as Mrs. Gemmer, whose *Babyland* was published in 1877. See above, Lttr. 38 and n. 2, and below, Lttr. 98.

72 ⋄ *Christina Rossetti to F. S. Ellis*

Text: British Museum MS. *Extracts published, TLS* (June 26, 1959), p. 389; *WHR* (Summer, 1962), p. 247.

56 Euston Square, N.W.

7th March 1870

Dear Sir

Your last letter has greatly obliged me and I thank you for the straightforward friendship of its tone. It certainly is not the case that my Nursery Rhymes were 'declined'; but perhaps as the business was not transacted immediately with Mr. Craik he <was not> though a partner,[1] was not aware of every detail. I am still waiting for a communication from Mr. Macmillan on the subject of Goblin Market, etc., but hope that it will not be very long before I can tell you more.

About the illustrations to the Nursery Rhymes my brother

Mr. Rossetti [2] wrote to me two days ago: 'S[cott] was mentioning to me an idea that Miss Boyd [3] would have been glad to put those things on the blocks for your Nursery Rhymes. I fancy she would really probably do them with more fun and zest than Murray though perhaps not so artistically— Her ideas for beast drawing are good as you know.' I just tell you this, though I fear it may be too late. Miss Boyd, who has exhibited more than once is a most particular friend of mine: <and it would have been very nice> but of course the point is for you conclusively to decide.

I understand from my brother that you would be likely to take a volume of short stories (prose) [4] if I got them ready, and as I hope soon to have enough for a small volume will send them to you to look at in due course.

Yours very truly,

Christina G. Rossetti

---

[1] George Lillie Craik (d. 1905), husband of the celebrated author of *John Halifax*, became a partner in 1865, "a fortunate choice," according to Morgan, for "though he had an artificial leg and other physical disabilities," Craik "was precisely what Alexander needed as an administrator—a man full of energy and character" (p. 69). He remained with the firm until his death and became a legend with the staff members. " 'Is you hearrrrt in your worrrrrk?' he would demand of them as he passed their desks." Macmillan wrote of him in 1873, "And dear Craik is so good and wise and careful and kind. I cannot tell you how I have got to love that man. He is a daily comfort and guide to me. . . ." (Graves, p. 316).

[2] DGR.

[3] Although W. B. Scott and Alice Boyd preserved the proprieties, theirs was, despite the existence of Mrs. Scott, "a perfect friendship" (Scott's term), on the order of George Eliot's with George Lewes. Scott spent his summers at Penkill Castle, Alice's seat in Ayrshire, and winters she resided with him and his wife first at Newcastle, later in London. The three Rossettis were frequently invited to Penkill Castle. For further information about the complex tangle of relationships within the circle, see my *Christina Rossetti*.

[4] On March 5 William wrote in his diary that Christina had "about finished a longish prose-story named *Commonplace* (I have not as yet

any very clear notion of its bearing): this, and other slighter stories of past time, she proposes to put together and get them published by Ellis—who seems quite ready to accept them" (*Ross. Pprs.*, p. 500).

73 ❖ *Christina Rossetti to D. G. Rossetti*
Text: Univ. Texas MS.

56 Euston Square
Monday morning [Spring, 1870] [1]

My dear Gabriel

Thank you for the hint about Miss Boyd. I have passed it on to Ellis, though too late perhaps (the work being already Murray's) to be acted on—of course leaving the decision to him. We are still waiting for a letter from Macmillan about the complete edition.

Your affectionate sister
C. G. Rossetti

---

[1] The square brackets are mine. I date the letter according to its obvious place in the series.

74 ❖ *Christina Rossetti to F. S. Ellis*
Text: British Museum MS. *Extract published, WHR* (Summer, 1962), p. 247.

56 Euston Square, N.W.
Saturday evening [March, 1870]

My dear Mr. Ellis

I am extremely pleased both that Mr. Murray should do some of my illustrations and that Miss Boyd should (if as I trust she will) undertake the rest. Her address is

33 Elgin Road
Notting Hill—W [1]

After what my brother has said it is needless for me to express admiration of her talents. I am sending her your note, so that if you open direct communications with her you will find the way paved: or perhaps she will write first to you. No, on second thought, I suppose she might prefer not writing first.

I hope very soon to send you my little prose volume, but have not quite finished copying the principal story. Mr. Macmillan has not written yet about the volume of verse. It struck me, after receiving the hint you kindly gave me as to utilizing the remaining copies of 'Goblin Market,' that after all I fear it will be impossible to incorporate them in an 'entire' edition: for it seems that <u>at most</u> not more than 450 copies remain on hand, and I suppose it might not answer to publish so small an edition as 450—besides the doubt whether there really are so many. In short I know not what to do about it all.

I let my friend—she lives in the country—know your answer about the cost of printing and publishing; and this morning I heard from her again begging me to oblige her by asking Mr. Ellis if he would "object to printing quite a miniature volume after the pattern (or as near as may be) of Mr. Bennett's 'Baby May'? If he entertains the notion I will send him 'Baby May' with such of my M.S. as I can endure to see in print for his printer to look over and make a calculation as to price, etc." She writes a good deal more, but I think this is all I need ask you to oblige us by answering to <u>me</u>: as if you say you would not object, I think she had better put herself in direct communication with you. She has already been in print two or three times; with volumes of verse, I mean, so is not a mere novice as an authoress.

Sincerely yours
Christina G. Rossetti

I believe Miss Boyd is so sure to undertake the 'SingSong' illustrations, that the sooner she has them in hand the better.

---

[1] Scott's London address.

75 ❖ *D. G. Rossetti to Christina*

Text: *Dante Gabriel Rossetti's Family Letters with a Memoir,* ed. W. M.
Rossetti (1895), II, 224. Second postscript omitted.

[SCALANDS, ROBERTSBRIDGE.]
Wednesday [23 March 1870].[1]

DEAR CHRISTINA

I have read *Commonplace* (which I return by bookpost),
and like it very much. It certainly is not dangerously exciting
to the nervous system, but it is far from being dull for all that,
and I should think it likely to take. Stillman and I noted one or
two trifles on the opposite blank pages for your consideration
—mere trifles. He likes it much also.

I return the MS. by bookpost. No doubt Ellis will be very
glad to have it as soon as you can let him. I am glad Miss Boyd
is to do the woodcuts.

Your affectionate
GABRIEL.

P.S.—Of course I think your proper business is to write
poetry, and not *Commonplaces.*

------

[1] William is responsible for the conjectural date. In a letter also dated
March 23, Gabriel wrote Ellis that he had read the leading tale of
Christina's volume and thought it "very good (in the Miss Austen vein
rather) and sure I should fancy of a good success" (Doughty, *Lttrs. to
Ellis,* pp. 14–15). Three days later he inquired of Ellis, "Have you read
my sister's stories, and how do you like them?" (*ibid.,* p. 16).

76 ❖ *Christina Rossetti to F. S. Ellis*

Text: British Museum MS.

56 Euston Square, N.W.
29th March 1870

Dear Mr. Ellis

I am very glad to close with your terms, if you end by offering them: 4th part down of the published price of 500 copies when the book is ready, and when these are sold some proportion of successive 250s.

I am so sorry you do not like the title 'Commonplace'—for what else to name the every-day story I know not. I have been turning titles over in my head at intervals all day, and can't think of one. One capital title did occur to my sister, 'Births, Deaths and Marriages'—but then we are not certain that some one has not already made use of it. If you do not recollect any book bearing the name, do you think we might risk it? No one character in the tale is so prominent as to give <u>her</u> name to it; and the same of the few simple incidents. As regards my writing an additional story to increase bulk, perhaps you with me will shrink from the expedient when I tell you that the 6 you have in hand are nearly all the prose I have written between '52 and '70! However I have 2 more trifles in print [1] (one not strictly a tale, but perhaps it might go in with the rest) which I will send you in case you may think them available and better than nothing: but unfortunately they are quite short. One I have by me, and I will send you both <as soon as> when I have got a copy of the other which I have ordered.

The appearance of my specimen page delighted me, and 320 pages far exceeded aught I had supposed possible: but <unfort> then of course I judge and admire as an amateur, and you demur as an adept.

Miss Boyd called here yesterday bringing us specimens of her charming designs.[2] I shall be extremely glad to see the proofs you promised me, and hope they will do justice to her drawings.

As to a general title for my prose vol. I thought of calling it
Commonplace
with
Other short stories
by
Christina Georgina Rossetti

82

Would that do, do you think? and I should probably want to add a motto.[3]

Yours very truly

Christina G. Rossetti

---

[1] The *Commonplace* volume consists of eight prose fiction pieces, including the title story. In 1867 there was some talk of Roberts Brothers bringing out six of them in a volume, but this was not done, and on April 12, Christina wrote to the Boston firm asking it to return the stories (Troxell, p. 155). The six she lists were undoubtedly those Ellis had in hand. They were "Hero," "Pros and Cons," "Nick," "The Lost Titian," "The Waves of this Troublesome World," and "Safe Investment." She was writing the title story in 1870 and possibly "Vanna's Twins" as well.

"Hero," published in *Argosy* (Jan., 1866, pp. 156–165), was considered "splendid" by Gabriel, and by Swinburne as an example of Christina's genius for writing "beautiful work" which would give "passionate delight to imaginative children" as well as "more articulate and expressible pleasure" to men (Lang, II, 101). "The Lost Titian" first appeared in *Crayon,* the American art journal edited by William Stillman. "Pros and Cons," "A Safe Investment," and "The Waves . . . etc." all were published in *Churchman's Shilling* in 1867 (I: 496–500 and 182–193, 291–304; II: 287–292). Swinburne called "Vanna's Twins" the "sweetest story of them all," but complained of Christina's cruelty in killing off the children: "After the delicious description of the babies, which made me purr with pleasure and feel as if my fur was being rubbed the right way, the blow of the catastrophe came on me almost like a physical shock" (Lang, II, 116).

[2] Alice Boyd's illustrations are still extant, in possession of Miss Evelyn Courtney-Boyd of Penkill Castle.

[3] "From sea to sea."

77 ❖ *Christina Rossetti to Alexander Macmillan*
Text: Macmillan MS. Published: *WHR* (Summer, 1962), p. 249.

56 Euston Square, N.W.

29th March 1870.

Dear Mr. Macmillan

I have been fancying you were going to write to me as the

83

result of my brother's calling on you, and I have not had a letter. So if I do not shortly hear from you I will conclude that the complete edition question has dropped for the present. My Nursery Rhymes are in hand and I hope promise to look pretty.

What a winter! this March is very like January. When will the world grow green again?

Sincerely yours
Christina G. Rossetti

78 ❖ Christina Rossetti to F. S. Ellis

Text: British Museum MS. *Extract published, WHR* (Summer, 1962), pp. 249–250.

56 Euston Square, N.W.
Wednesday evening [April, 1870]

Dear Mr. Ellis

Thank you sincerely. We will, if you please, make Mr. Charlmont [1] 'come' unexpectedly into some hundreds a 'year' p.q. As to his speculations, I imagine him doing such things as buying in and selling out at lucky moments, though not otherwise than as a perfectly upright man may do. Do you think this too much, or that my word does not convey my meaning? If the latter, I bow to your superior business knowledge, and will let <him> it be that he 'invested his savings profitably.' [2]

As the proof in question has passed for the last time through my hands I am sure I may trust this furthest revision to your kindness.

Sincerely yours,
Christina G. Rossetti

---

[1] Father of Lucy Charlmont, heroine of *Commonplace*.

[2] "Mr. Charlmont died a wealthy man. He had enjoyed a large lucrative practice, and had invested his savings profitably: by his will, and on their mother's death, an ample provision remained for his daughters" (*Commonplace*, 1870, p. 16).

79 ❖ *Christina Rossetti to F. S. Ellis*

Text: British Museum MS. Published: *WHR* (Summer, 1962), p. 250.

56 Euston Square, N.W.

Friday 29th [April, 1870]

Dear Mr. Ellis

I do not know whether it is monstrous to imagine you wasting 4 o'clock next Tuesday afternoon on a kettledrum; but I should like our acquaintance to get beyond knowing each other's handwriting by sight, and I hope a few kind friends will favour us at the time indicated. The week following I expect to leave town.

If I blunder in asking you pray pardon

Yours truly

Christina G. Rossetti

80 ❖ *Christina Rossetti to F. S. Ellis*

Text: British Museum MS.

56 Euston Square, N.W.

Saturday night [April 30, 1870]

Dear Mr. Ellis

I send my receipt and my thanks for the handsome checque you so kindly sent me before it falls due, and heartily join in your hope for your sake as well as for my own that 'Commonplace' may sell.

I look forward with real pleasure to our chance of seeing you next Tuesday when you will find Miss Boyd amongst our small circle of friends.[1]

Very truly yours

Christina G. Rossetti

---

[1] The tea represents the high point in the Rossetti-Ellis relationship. Ellis was publishing *Commonplace* and Gabriel's *Poems* and was going ahead with *Sing-Song*. The first edition of 1,000 copies of Gabriel's volume sold out within a week of publication date (April 25), and Ellis went to press with the second thousand copies.

Aside from the obvious place of this letter in the sequence, its conjectural date may be confirmed by Mrs. Rossetti's note to Gabriel May 6, 1870, telling him she had met Ellis, who was "a fine looking Englishman" (Bodleian, Ross. MS 22).

81 ❖ *Christina Rossetti to F. S. Ellis*

Text: British Museum MS.

56 Euston Square, N.W.
Saturday night [May, 1870]

Dear Mr. Ellis

Pray alter the title page as you suggest and with my entire good will. May it aid our sale and disarm my critics. I hope the 250 will do no harm.

Thank you for my prospective copy.[1] I shall be particularly obliged if you can let me have 12 copies more, and also let me know how much they leave me in your debt next Monday; as I leave town for some little time on Tuesday.

Sincerely yours,
Christina G. Rossetti

---

[1] *Commonplace* was published May 7.

82 ❖ *F. S. Ellis to Alice Boyd*

Text: Penkill Library MS A 10.

33 King Street
Covent Garden
May 14, 1870

Dear Miss Boyd

I have sent you by this post some further proofs but I think they have not sent you the improved proof of the 3 angels watching. Will you kindly send me the MS. of the verses you have done with as I should like to get the type set up and see how the blocks look as they are printed by my printer. The baby in the cradle appears to me to be very much better than in the first proof. You will be glad to hear that Gabriel Rossetti's Poems are quite out of print. The new edition is in hand and will I hope be ready by next Friday.

Trusting that you arrived quite safely at your destination,[1] believe me

Dear Miss Boyd
Yours faithfully
F. S. Ellis

---

[1] Penkill Castle, Girvan, Ayrshire.

83 ❖ F. S. Ellis to Alice Boyd

Text: Penkill Library MS A 10.

35 King Street
Covent Garden
May 25, 1870

Dear Miss Boyd

I am really quite ashamed to think how long I have left your letter unanswered. First Mr. [illegible] tells me that he can materially improve the child's face in No. 83 which is satisfactory to know. I will send you proofs of the others and will you let me know when you would like some more of the plates to be sent to you? I have been so very much engaged with a variety of things that I have not been able to give this book so much attention as I ought to have done. I spoke this morning about the proof of the angels and child<ren> and they promise to let me have an improved proof directly.[1] I can easily believe how much you must enjoy the lovely country— no one can love the country more heartily than I do and the only way I can keep myself from feeling miserable is to determine not to think of it at this time of the year—to regard it simply as one of the unattainable things of life, as one might dream of possessing a Carpaccio or Leonardo picture.

You will be glad to hear that Rossetti's book continues to

sell—to say that it has far exceeded my expectations would
be a moderate phrase to use.[2] Believe me Dear Miss Boyd

Yours faithfully

F. S. Ellis

---

[1] "Ellis has not sent for the parcel," Scott wrote Alice Boyd on May
30, "but I do nothing as you have written about it. At the same time
it has now lain here you know nearly three weeks" (Penkill Lib. MS,
uncatalogued).

[2] On May 24 Ellis inserted in *The Pall Mall Gazette* a large advertisement of the second edition of Gabriel's *Poems;* on the 28th a similar
advertisement appeared of the third edition.

84 ❖ *Christina Rossetti to F. S. Ellis*

Text: British Museum MS. *Extracts published, TLS* (June 26, 1959), p.
389; *WHR* (Summer, 1962), p. 251.

56 Euston Square, N.W.

1st June 1870

Dear Mr. Ellis

I enclose a P.O.O. for the money portion of my debt to
you, cordially acknowledging the liberality with which you
have all along treated me. Pray believe that my wish for some
commercial success with both my volumes regards your interest
as well as my own. I still hope that favourable reviews may
rescue 'Commonplace' from oblivion; but am sorry to say I
know not of any such definite prospect, beyond a rumour that
the 'Pall Mall' means to treat me well.[1] However, I trust it
is not yet too late for hope.

I ventured to mention my brother Gabriel's remarks to you;
but certainly I do not venture to urge them, sharing, as I do,
neither risk nor responsibility. It strikes me that if anything
could be done to lessen the evil we both perceive, it might be
to suggest to Miss Boyd to make no more large figure designs;
thus the bulk of the illustrations might be rescued from the
misfortune which has already befallen some: but I merely
mention this as what has occurred to me. Now pray allow me

to mention something of more importance. I can readily imagine that if 'Commonplace' proves a total failure, 'Sing-Song' may dwindle to a very serious risk: and therefore I beg you at once, if you deem the step prudent, to put a stop to all further outlay on the rhymes, until you can judge whether my name is marketable. It would probably not be long before you could give me a final answer as to 'Sing-Song,' after which of course I should be at liberty to try its fortunes elsewhere, if I thought it worth while.

Congratulating you on the marked success of my brother's volume, I remain

Always truly yours

Christina G. Rossetti

---

[1] Ellis advertised *Commonplace* in both *The Pall Mall Gazette* (May 24 and 28) and *The Athenæum* (May 14); and consequently these periodicals gave the volume some attention. Probably DGR's literary friends who launched his *Poems* with such striking success also took a hand in reviewing his sister's book. Sidney Colvin, who praised DGR's *Poems* in *The Pall Mall Gazette,* may have written for the same journal the June 7 review of *Commonplace,* which begins, "The lady who with her two previous volumes, 'Goblin Market' and 'The Prince's Progress,' has won for herself an undisputed place among the poets of her day, comes with the present volume to claim a place also among its prose writers." After summarizing the events in the title piece, the reviewer observes that "in all this there is little room for the exciting elements of fiction. The story is one that must depend upon tranquil description and the delineation of everyday character; upon those qualities of quiet humour and insight which alone can give relief where there is no colour." Although he goes on to praise the "terseness" of Miss Rossetti's prose style, one of its "major merits," and her "subdued intensity of manner," he concludes that "in the art of painting with moral grays, Miss Rossetti here shows a proficiency which is best compared with Mrs. Gaskell," a verdict likely to chill the prospective buyer's interest.

The Athenæum, then edited by Norman McColl, had already published Christina's poetry and was to publish more of her work. A contributor for some twenty-five years (1870–1895), William was on the staff during 1881, reviewing some five or six books a year, seldom more. This journal's review of *Commonplace*—"slipshod but quotable," said Gabriel—may have been written by Philip Bourke Marston, the blind poet who reviewed Gabriel's *Poems* for *The Athenæum*. Likewise comparing Christina's title story to Mrs. Gaskell's *Cranford,* the reviewer recommends it as a "homely" antidote to the brilliant sensationalism of Mr. Disraeli's "tawdry romance" *Lothair* (June 4, pp. 734–735), again not the kind of criticism calculated to bring the volume that "commercial success" Christina wished for it.

85 ⬦ *Christina Rossetti to F. S. Ellis*
Text: British Museum MS. *Extracts published, TLS* (June 26, 1959), p. 389; *WHR* (Summer, 1962), p. 253.

2 [Copt] Hall Place
Folkstone
Wednesday morning [Summer, 1870] [1]

Dear Mr. Ellis

I am so sorry for all the money you have spent on Sing-Song, which may well hide its diminished head for one while. If ever its publication comes in question again, do you think it would be worth while doing what Gabriel thinks feasible? omitting the ugly human beings, but making use of the pretty beasts and flowers. Thank you gratefully for not mentioning my name, though if the slightest difficulty as to truth arises I beg you to bring me in unsparingly even to Miss Boyd.

I have not seen the Ch[urchman's] Shilling Magazine, and should have supposed it might have had a warm word for me.[2] Pazienza!

No, I went by the *Sunday Times,*[3] *Graphic, Guardian,* and a few others which you probably know. Still I am glad that even so many, though so few, copies have sold. We are not all D.G.R.s.

Sincerely yours
Christina G. Rossetti

---

[1] The reference to the reviews and Gabriel's 1870 *Poems* places the letter in the summer of 1870 rather than 1871. Although Christina was in Folkestone both years, by 1871 Routledge was publishing *Sing-Song* and her letters from Folkestone discuss proofs. See below, Lttr. 89, and *Fam. Lttrs.,* pp. 32, 34, and 35.

² I could find no review in *Churchman's Shilling,* which in 1867 had published three of the stories (see above, Lttr. 76 and n. 1).

³ Christina could have had no cause to complain of the discerning criticism in *The Sunday Times* (June 12, p. 7), of which Joseph Knight (1829–1907), Gabriel's first biographer, was editor, though even here the writer did her the same disservice as the other reviewers in comparing her volume to more exciting literature, in this case to French novels. "We can liken the sensation upon reading the book to a draught of pure water to one who has drunk of fiery vintages. . . ." But after this initial rhetorical flourish, the reviewer selects as the most characteristic feature of Christina's prose fiction its poetic quality, that is, "the delicacy and purity of workmanship, the tenderness and the grace that have again and again charmed in 'The Goblin Market' and 'The Prince's Progress,' and in poem after poem which has appeared in magazine and serial." Alighting upon the happy phrase, "a gilded commonplace," he observes that "with no great difficulty we could fancy the object of the story to be to prove that in life there is no commonplace. . . . The tragic element in human life saves the humblest existence from absolute commonplace." The volume, all in all, he concludes, is "an intellectual treat of no common description."

86 ❖ *D. G. Rossetti to Alexander Macmillan*

16 Cheyne Walk
30 Dec 1870

Dear Macmillan

As there are so many Goblin Markets, will you kindly send me one. My messenger must have spoken to some one who didn't know, as he was certainly told that both books were out of print and reprinting.¹ He is much too unimaginative to have conceived the idea.

I shall be very glad to see yourself, son, and all friends, some time in March, but till then shall be completely boxed up with a big picture I am doing.² It & I have now been tugging against each other for some months, but I mean to get it under by then. Bye the bye, my dear Macmillan, it is all very well talking about "Fame in the next generation," but why does your magazine resolutely ignore the best things going? It's no business & no meaning of mine to speak for myself—let anyone do that who pleases—but why in the world has Morris been left in the lurch till now?[3] I don't know who your present editor is,[4] but I may assure him that it is of no use sulking over good work. There is some credit in acknowledging it at first; and it has to be acknowledged at last without credit at all. So for my New Year's gift of plain speech to your publication.

To yourself & to yours come all good & seasonable wishes from

Yours always
DG Rossetti

---

[1] See above, Lttr. 77.

[2] *Dante's Dream,* completed about November, 1871.

[3] In 1870 William Morris had finished *The Earthly Paradise,* and with Magnússon had translated the *Volsunga Saga.* Although Morris was painting and illuminating, according to Mackail he was more or less at loose ends, wavering "between an instinct to break new ground in poetry and a reaction from the immense production of the last three years." (*The Life of William Morris,* World Classics ed., 2 vols., 1899, I, 215.)

[4] George Grove (1820–1900) edited the *Magazine* from 1867 to 1883, when he was appointed the first director of the Royal College of Music. The firm published his great *Dictionary of Music and Musicians,* 4 vols. (1877–1889).

87 ❖ *Christina Rossetti to F. S. Ellis*
Text: British Museum MS.

56 Euston Square, N.W.
2nd March 1871

Dear Mr. Ellis

I am unfortunately obliged once more to trouble you about *SingSong.* This morning I looked through the Rhymes with an eye to business, and was very sorry to find 22 of them missing. I am sure of this because the whole set is numbered in sequence. The strayed nos are: 5—11—13—16—17—18—20—21—23—31—37—42—43—47—55—60—70—73—83—88—89.

Would it be possible for you to recover them anywhere and restore them to me? I fear my poor little book is troublesome to you <nearly> even as it were in its grave; but pray believe me that it is so quite against my will. I should like as soon as well may be to hear from you on the subject.

Very truly yours

Christina G. Rossetti

88 ✧ *Christina Rossetti to* [*Dalziel Brothers*] [1]

Text: Univ. Texas MS.

56 Euston Square—N.W.

26 April 1871.

Dear Sirs

I gladly agree to the terms you propose and will send you a formal note to that effect, if you will first inform me whom you intend employing to design the illustrations and if of course the name pleases me. There is also a preliminary question I am putting to Mr. Niles as to Messrs. Roberts' terms,[2] but this I dare say will cause no delay in our dealings.

I should enjoy seeing my specimen pages, and may have that pleasure if they can be looked at before the 4th of May. But on that day I expect to leave town, and if I have not then seen them my brother William Rossetti kindly undertakes to be the consulting party in my stead. He is at home most evenings after 6.30, and will settle everything for me.

Sincerely yours

Christina G. Rossetti

P.S. Of course I trust you will let me have my proofs for correction.[3]

[illegible]	Animals and Birds
Solman [4]	Flowers
Fraser	Figures

The above names were suggested to Miss Rossetti as suitable artists to illustrate her book but the selection ultimately fell upon Mr. Arthur Hughes[5] who very successfully carried out the author's wishes.

Dalziel Brothers

---

[1] The Dalziel Brothers, who added the list of names and the explanatory note, were obviously the recipients of the letter. See above, Lttr. 49, n. 1.

[2] See above, Lttr. 53, n. 2.

[3] Despite frightening attacks of her illness, which periodically tightened and relaxed its grip, Christina prepared her book for publication, even to the nerve-trying ordeal of proofreading.

[4] This might be Simeon Soloman with the second "o" left out.

[5] Arthur Hughes (1832–1915), third and final illustrator for the book, which was published by Routledge in November, 1871. "Christina's book," Dante Gabriel wrote Swinburne, "is I think divinely lovely, both in itself and in Arthur Hughes' illustrations which are quite unequalled for sweetness" (Brit. Mus. MS Ash. 4995, p. xxxv).

89 ❖ *Christina Rossetti to* [*Dalziel Brothers*]
Text: Univ. Texas MS.

5 Gloucester Place—Folkestone.
3rd August 1871.

Dear Sirs

I hope the "press" sheets are not inconveniently delayed through their having had to follow me here. The new sheets (for revise) keep up to the mark, and altogether the cuts deserve to sell the volume. Would it—it strikes me that it might—be attractive to print "Arthur Hughes" in larger type in the titlepage? We shall certainly owe so much to him.

For the present I must ask you kindly to forward proofs to me here at Folkestone, whither my Doctor has sent me to recruit; but already I am much better.

Very truly yours
Christina G. Rossetti

56 Euston Sq. N.W.
5 Novr. [1871] [1]

Dear Macmillan

The other day I received a little account from you for 3 copies of my Inferno supplied on my order: also a trifle for postage. I am not entirely clear how this matter stands. As the Inferno was published at my own cost, & as I paid some while ago (I think at the close of 1868) your claim in respect of its publication [? fee], I had supposed that the remaining stock is now my personal property; that any copies sold to extraneous persons were so much recouping to me of my expenses; & that any supplied on my order were free from cost either way— or only subject to a percentage receivable by you as transacting the delivery. Wd. you kindly let me know how this really stands: also whether any copies, other than the 3 named in your present account, have been sold since I discharged your original claim on the publication. I cd. call some afternoon if more satisfactory.

I much regretted to receive not very long ago the notice of your sorrowful bereavement.[2] In this house of late there has been much sickness—Christina entirely prostrated for mos., & still in a state causing great distress & anxiety.[3]

Yours very truly
W. M. Rossetti

Perhaps you wd. add, to the details about the Inferno, any (if any there are) as to the book on Fine Art.

---

[1] Year date by the firm.

[2] The death of the first Mrs. Macmillan, the former Caroline Brimley, which occurred in July, 1871.

[3] In 1871–1872 CGR was seriously ill with Graves' disease (exophthalmic goiter), a disorder which impaired her good looks and caused her great suffering. See introduction to this section and below, Lttr. 99. See also Troxell, pp. 106–107, and for a detailed account of CGR's illness *Christina Rossetti*, pp. 284–295.

56 Euston Square—N.W.

1st December 1871

Dear Mr. Macmillan

I received with surprise this evening a little sum on my *Goblin Market* about which I no longer thought at all as a source of profit. Thank you, and please accept my receipt <appended> enclosed. I am sorry to see so many Goblins still in the market, as otherwise the small remainder of Prince's Progress we could have dealt with.[1]

If you have seen SingSong I hope you have admired the beautiful illustrations which charm my brother Dante.[2]

Very sincerely yours

Christina G. Rossetti

---

[1] See above, Lttrs. 77 and 86.
[2] See Lttr. 88, n. 5.

1874–1876

The letters of these years fall into three main groups: those concerned with Macmillan's publication of Christina's *Speaking Likenesses* (1874), the ones dealing with the preparation, publication, and reviews of her collected poems (1875), and finally William's letters to Grove on the subject of his article, "William Bell Scott and Modern British Poetry," published in *Macmillan's Magazine* (March, 1876).

92 ❖ *Christina Rossetti to Alexander Macmillan*

Text: Macmillan MS. *Extract published, TLS* (June 5, 1959), p. 337.

56 Euston Square—N.W.

3 February 1874.

Dear Mr. Macmillan

I have tried to write a little prose story, such as might I think do for a child's Xmas volume, & if you would allow me to send it you to be looked at you would truly oblige me. Properly speaking, it consists of 3 short stories in a common framework,—but the whole is not long.[1]

A statement received a short time from your office shows me that Goblin Market is not so very far apparently from selling off,—& glad I am: also, of the 5-9-0 in prospect, especially as I have just now a wedding present to make.[2]

I like the opening of Castle Daly, though I must not expect it to equal the charming Princess of Thule.[3]

Very sincerely yours

Christina G. Rossetti

---

[1] This was *Speaking Likenesses* (1874), which Christina described as "merely a Christmas trifle, would-be in the *Alice* style with an eye to the market" (*Fam. Lttrs.*, p. 44). See "Not All Roses in the Victorian Nursery," *TLS*, Children's Book Section (May 29, 1959), and my comment (June 5), p. 337.

[2] For William and Lucy Brown, who married March 31, 1874. The sum "in prospect" was probably for CGR's poem *A Dirge* (*Works*, p. 379), published in the *Magazine* (Jan., 1874), p. 25.

[3] Annie Keary, *Castle Daly: the Story of an Irish Home Thirty Years Ago*, 3 vols. (1875), ran serially in abridged form in *Macmillan's Maga-*

zine from 1873 to 1875. *The Princess of Thule* (1874) was by William Black (1841–1898), a popular Scottish novelist, whose numerous works of fiction Macmillan published in book form and serialized in the *Magazine*. Black wrote the *Goldsmith* in John Morley's *English Men of Letters* series started by Macmillan in 1877.

93 ◆ *Christina Rossetti to Alexander Macmillan*

56 Euston Square—N.W.
4 February. 1874

Dear Mr. Macmillan

Thank you very much. Here is my little story on trial.

Will you think me too eccentric for returning—but with cordial sense of your liberal kindness—your cheque (herein) for 15£, & begging you to favour me by substituting one for that precise £5-9-0 which is all that I have earned? [1] I have more than enough for my wedding present, & like to feel that in the future an odd sovereign or two may now & then drop in.

The possibility of your thinking proper some day to reprint my 2 vols. in one, is really gratifying to me as you may suppose: but as to additional matter, I fear there will be little indeed to offer you. The fire has died out, it seems; & I know of no bellows potent to revive dead coals. I wish I did.

Very truly yours
Christina G. Rossetti

---

[1] William disapproved of what he called his sister's "overscrupulosity," the "one serious flaw in a beautiful and admirable character" (*Works*, pp. lxvii–lxviii), possibly because on occasion he himself suffered from it (see above, Lttr. 48). At one time she offered to return to "the *Century* 'magnates'" the twenty guineas they had paid her for an article about Dante (February, 1884) if it should occur to the editors that they had overpaid her.

56 Euston Square—N.W.

20 April 1874.

Dear Mr. Macmillan

I am glad to accept your offer for Nowhere,[1] not having expected such success with you just now. The only supplementary point I should like to suggest would be that we fix a time by which it is to be published, & after which in want of non-publication the copyright simply without any further process reverts to me. Suppose we say it shall be out on or before the 31st December of this year:—otherwise, etc.

About illustrations. Nothing would please me more than Mr. Arthur Hughes

(2 Finborough Road

Fulham Road—S.W.)

should do them. His in my SingSong were reckoned charming by Gabriel, not to speak of other verdicts. This would give me pleasure, but of course the question is yours & not mine. Another who I fancy might like to undertake them & do them very well, would be Mr. Smetham.[2] I do not know where he lives, but of course could find out.

Really pleased, & thanking you for all kind good will in our family matters,

Very sincerely yours

Christina G. Rossetti

I dare say you will favour me with a word of reply, acquainting me with your decision.[3]

---

[1] "Nowhere" was the projected title of *Speaking Likenesses.*

[2] See above, Lttr. 57 and n. 1.

[3] On May 4 CGR wrote DGR, "Do you see (what I am told through two or three reporters, for I have not myself seen it) that *The Athenæum* has announced a story of mine to come out with Macmillan? Funnily enough, I did not know matters were concluded between Mac and me, but now I hope they are" (*Fam. Lttrs.,* pp. 43–44).

95 ❖ *Christina Rossetti to Alexander Macmillan*

Text: Macmillan MS. *Extract published, TLS* (June 5, 1959), p. 337.

All Saints Hospital—Eastbourne
Monday 27. July [1874] [1]

Dear Mr. Macmillan

Please observe my address till, I think, the 20th of next month. Not, indeed, a very momentous announcement, except that you may recollect I am hoping some day to receive my revise with all its pretty pictures.

And then I really must adopt "Speaking Likenesses" as my title, this having met with some approval in my circle. Very likely you did not so deeply ponder upon my text as to remark that my small heroines perpetually encounter "speaking (literally speaking) likenesses" or embodiments or caricatures of themselves or their faults. This premised, I think the title boasts of some point & neatness.

Do you know anything of this grand Hospital where my Mother & I are staying? [2] We, of course, as paying visitors: but (say) 200 other poor people, convalescents, enjoying all comforts within this magnificent house, & without superb sea & downs to their hearts' content. This is truly a noble institution, worthy of support on all hands as patients are admitted to it from all parts,—& reflecting high honour on its Foundress.

Very sincerely yours
Christina G. Rossetti

---

[1] Year date by firm.

[2] Macmillan visited Eastbourne with his family in 1861, but the Hospital was not opened until 1869. Started by the Anglican Sisterhood of All Saints', Margaret Street, Cavendish Square, of which the first Mother Superior, Harriet Brownlow Byron (1818-1887) was the foundress, the Hospital had the distinction of being the first seaside convalescent home in England and the first hospital of its kind founded by an English religious order.

In 1874 Maria Rossetti (see above, Lttr. 29, n. 2) joined the Margaret Street Sisterhood, which as a nursing order worked closely with the

101

Rossettis' family physician, Sir William Jenner, at the University College Hospital, Gower Street. Already suffering from the internal tumor which caused her death in 1876, during her novitiate, Maria was a frequent patient at Eastbourne, where she was occasionally visited by Christina and their mother. Chiefly remembered for *A Shadow of Dante* (1871), Maria translated for the order the Day Hours of the Roman Breviary, which was re-issued in 1923 as *A Book of Day Hours for the Use of Religious Societies,* and is a standard work. See Peter F. Anson, *The Call of the Cloister* (1955), pp. 317–327.

96 ❖ *W. M. Rossetti to Alexander Macmillan*

56 Euston Sq. N.W.
29 Oct. /74.

Dear Macmillan,

A friend of mine spoke to me yesterday about a M.S. by a friend of his (to me unknown)—a son of the Profr. Ferrier who married a daughter of Profr. Wilson.[1] The M.S. is a translation of Heinrich Heine's Essay on the Romantic School; & if I understood my friend aright, Mr. Ferrier has also translated & wishes to publish various others of Heine's prose-works. I am told that it is really an object to him to find a publisher from whom some sum of money wd. be forthcoming.

I have looked a little at the M.S. of the Romantic School, & it seems to me to be executed with the requisite amount of ability.

Do you think it wd. suit you to publish this Essay or others of the Heine translations of Mr. Ferrier? May I send you the M.S. wh. is at present in my hands? One thing I feel pretty certain of—that you, as a compatriot of Wilson's wd. be pleased to do anything beneficial to a connection of his.

With best regards
Very truly yours,
W. M. Rossetti

The essay on the Romantic School must no doubt be a work of great literary interest & importance. I believe it is a fact that this & other prose writings of Heine have never yet been produced in English.[2]

---

[1] James Frederick Ferrier (1808–1864) was the well-known philosopher and Professor of Moral Philosophy at St. Andrews. John Wilson (1785–1854), Professor of Moral Philosophy at Edinburgh, contributed to *Blackwood's* under the name of Christopher North. Professor Ferrier edited his *Works* (1855–1858). I find no record of Ferrier's son or the publication of his translation of Heine's "Essay" in the *Macm. Bib. Cat.* However, in 1881, 1883, and 1884 Macmillan published translations from other of Heine's prose writings, none of them by Ferrier.

[2] The first English translation of Heine's prose works to be published was S. L. Fleishman's *Prose Miscellanies* (New York, 1876). The publishing house of Holt brought out a separate edition of Fleishman's translation of *The Romantic School* (New York, 1882). In 1887 Havelock Ellis edited Heine's *Prose Writings,* which included a translation of *The Romantic School.*

97 ❖ *Christina Rossetti to Alexander Macmillan*

Text: Macmillan MS. *Extract published, TLS* (June 5, 1959), p. 337.

56 Euston Square—N.W.
Friday evening [Autumn 1874][1]

Dear Mr. Macmillan

Thank you cordially for my book which pleases me much, & of which your gift of 6 copies was most welcome. I only hope the public appetite will not be satisfied with 6 or 60, but crave on for 600 or 6000 at least!

But Gabriel writes me that I ought to beg a <u>cancel</u> of the <u>titlepage</u>: & though I don't know how to ask this of you, I will own that "with pictures thereof" is so different from the "with (so many) illustrations" which I had thought of, that I feel uneasiness at the different form being read as my own. I don't think "thereof" happy in this particular context. Then the <u>List of Illustrations</u> treats my subjects as I should not have treated them: the word "fairy" I should altogether have excluded as not appropriate to my story,— I should have aimed at greater neatness & brevity,—& not least I should (as who would not?) have described the last on the list in other terms. In short, I am now deploring that the Titlepage & List of Illustrations were not shown me in proof, even if in the first instance I was not called upon to supply the latter.

What shall we do? Cannot something be done to remedy these oversights & soothe my anxiety? [2]

Do please reassure

Yours in trouble
Christina G. Rossetti

---

[1] Macmillan or the firm dates this letter 1875, but it was certainly written in the autumn of 1874 when *Speaking Likenesses* was published. See *Fam. Lttrs.*, pp. 47–48.

[2] Nothing was done. "With Pictures Thereof by Arthur Hughes" remains on the title page. The objectionable word "fairy" occurs as follows in the list of illustrations: "The Cross Fairy deprives Flora of her strawberry feast." In Christina's story it is the arrogant Birthday Queen, not a cross fairy, who snatches away the small heroine's strawberry (pp. 23–24, 26). The wording of the last on the list reads, "Maggie drinks tea and eats buttered toast with Granny," not inspired diction, certainly.

98 ❖ *Christina Rossetti to Alexander Macmillan*

56 Euston Square—N.W.
Friday, 22nd January 1875.

Dear Mr. Macmillan

My friend Mrs. Gemmer, "Gerda Fay" in old days, & whose name might introduce her to you without any introduction from myself,—yet asks me to ascertain whether you will be disposed to look at the M.S. of a volume of verses for children she has by her, all complete & needing publication.[1] They seem to me to have a share of takingness which may make way for them when once brought before the public: but I own I am no judge of probable popularity in my own case!

What I am asking is the favour of your answer whether I

may forward for your verdict my friend's M.S. which is now in my hands: yes?—

Another time I shall hope to hear from you what fate has befallen *Speaking Likenesses,* but I will not mix up my own affairs with hers into one obscure confusion.

Hoping for your reply
Very sincerely yours
Christina G. Rossetti

---

[1] Having tried Ellis without success, CGR was probably endeavoring to interest Macmillan in Mrs. Gemmer's *Babyland,* finally published in 1877 (see above, Lttr. 71, n. 2).

99 ❖ *Christina Rossetti to Alexander Macmillan*
Text: Macmillan MS. *Extract published, TLS* (June 5, 1959), p. 337.

56 Euston Square—N.W.
26 January 1875.

Dear Mr. Macmillan

Thank you for answering me & my Friend so fully. I dare say she will succeed elsewhere, as her new volume seems to me to have merit: meanwhile we are obliged to you for letting us know her doom without delay, & I am glad to have attempted for her the very little which lay in my power.

To lapse to the private & personal. I am glad if there is any prospect of another edition of my verses being wanted some day, & one nice fattish volume takes my fancy. Have any more of the last copies of "Goblin Market" sold? I have not received the usual statement this Xmas, as you may recollect.

I am pleased to hear of more than 1000 "Speaking Likenesses" having been disposed of: truth to tell, I had feared the reviews might this time have done me a very real injury with the buying public; but, for me, such a sale is certainly not bad.[1] I have been thinking over the terms you originally offered me & which were settled between us, that I should have 35£ & no further property or interest in the book: so I understood the arrangement to stand. Well, at this point of partial success, perhaps I may fairly suggest that if after all you should prefer our returning to our old system of half profits—the profits at this moment being for aught I know O.—I shall be most happy to fall back on those familiar terms, & run the risk of something or nothing as the case may be. I may get more, I know, by some incalculable contingency; but I count on no such result: I may equally get less or get nothing. In short, if you <like present> leave present terms to stand, I shall like my 35£: or if you change to halves, I shall like them perhaps on the whole better. (Very likely such a suggestion is simply monstrous from a business point of view: but if so, I am sure you are enough my kind friend to excuse my business ignorance.)

Now let us get away from the fog of business into the sunshine of pleasure. I hope that much health & enjoyment awaits you & Mrs. Macmillan in our lovely Italy. Pray assure her that I do not forget having, when she was Miss Pignatel,[2] once met her & her Sister at my kind friends' the Leifchilds':[3] but I have since then gone through so much illness as may suffice to colour soberly the rest of my days; & what with one thing & another, I am now disposed to ask rather that some who kindly recollect me should continue their remembrance, than that they should re-admit me of [sic] their acquaintance. Will she then, & will you, accept my very cordial compliments in lieu of my visit?

Always & very sincerely yours
Christina G. Rossetti

---

[1] "Miss Rossetti's are pretty, fanciful little stories, which would have been more original if Alice had never been to Wonderland," wrote the reviewer for *The Athenæum* (Dec. 27, 1874, pp. 878–879), admitting, however, that the title story was "well-conceived," and the last of the three tales "delightful."

Although granting that Christina's would probably be "one of the most popular children's books this winter," *The Academy* received it even more coolly, the reviewer writing in the December 6 issue, "We wish we could understand it . . . we have an uncomfortable feeling that a great deal more is meant than appears on the surface, and that every part of it ought to mean something if we only knew what it was." It is true that there is much symbolism in these stories of the kind found in Christina's poetry, a fact perceived and commented upon by the writer of "Not All Roses in the Victorian Nursery" (see above, Lttr. 92, n. 1).

[2] Macmillan's first wife having died in 1871 (see above, Lttr. 90, n. 2), the following autumn he married Emma Pignatel, a former schoolmate of his children's governess. Since the second Mrs. Macmillan's parents were Italian, this led to his making his first visit to Italy in 1873, in which "he found such keen pleasure that it was repeated more than once in later years" (*Macm. Lttrs.*, Glasgow ed., p. xlvii).

[3] The Leifchild brothers, Henry and Franklin, were friends of Christina's admirer, Charles Bagot Cayley.

100 ❖ *Christina Rossetti to Alexander Macmillan*

56 Euston Square—N.W.
30 January 1875.

Dear Mr. Macmillan

I am well contented, & send receipts & thanks.

By all means let us take in hand, if you please, a general reprint of my verses, fusing all into 1 volume. On the old terms of contingent half profits for me, & the copyright retained by me. So soon as I hear from you quite conclusively, I will look up what waifs & strays I can from Magazines, & forward them to you: of never-printed pieces, I fear I shall scarcely find one or two for use.[1] I shall like to make the arrangement of pieces carefully for myself, & suppose the fresh matter had better be introduced amongst the old, as suits subjects or what not. Of course I like to correct my own proofs, as heretofore: an author's privilege I cling to.

Very sincerely yours
Christina G. Rossetti

---

[1] Miss G. M. Hatton, who edited CGR's early unpublished poetry (St. Hilda's College, Oxford, 1955, unpub. B. Litt. diss.), was puzzled by the large number of poems Christina left unpublished in her life-

time, 350 according to Miss Hatton's count. Although William published most of them posthumously, a few complete poems and a number of suppressed stanzas remain in manuscript (see above, Lttr. 9, n. 2). Miss Hatton observes that "in contrast to many of the published poems, the original versions are much more personal in tone, reveal a wider range of mood and less inhibited reactions to experience, and indicate more clearly the conflicts arising out of self-doubt and faith, enjoyment and rejection of present pleasures. Some of the revisions must have also been made, partly at least, to conceal matters relating to private experiences" (p. lxxviii). See my *Christina Rossetti.*

101 ❖ *Christina Rossetti to Alexander Macmillan*

56 Euston Square—N.W.
25th March 1875.

Dear Mr. Macmillan

I dare say you are still enjoying your lovely Italian tour, & I hope it is giving you & yours much ennobling pleasure: pray offer my remembrances to Mrs. Macmillan.

I must write to the Firm, however, without waiting for your return, because of the letter which I enclose & which explains itself. I dare say I may count on your obliging me with proof sheets for Messrs. Roberts: may I not? & so excluding any rival edition from the U.S.A.[1] And if so, I am sure you will favour me by letting me have a proof of the 1st sheet for them, tho' this has already passed thro' my hands,—as well as of the others.

Thanking you for the anticipated favour to them & to myself
Very sincerely yours
Christina G. Rossetti.

---

[1] The problem of piracy by American publishers of English books was much discussed in the 1870's and early 1880's. Macmillan, a staunch defender of author's rights (see below, Lttr. 129, n. 1), published in the *Magazine* an article called, "The Ethics of Copyright" (Dec., 1880, pp. 153–160), in which the writer, Grant Allen, complained of "the great American nation" which permitted its publishers to "rob outright" the English writer, who thereby failed to derive any "pecuniary advantage

from the sale of his works across the Atlantic" (p. 156). But see "International Copyright with America," *Ath.* (July 10, 1875), p. 52.

Much the same position—as Allen's—was taken by American authors and responsible American publishers. In "The Copyright Negotiation," *Century* (March, 1882, pp. 667–671), Arthur G. Sedgewick ridiculed the chief argument put forward by the opponents of international copyright, that the advancement of learning in the United States depended upon cheap pirated books; and Edward Eggleston, in an article ironically entitled "The Blessings of Piracy," appearing in the same periodical (April, 1882, pp. 943–945), pointed out that the American author was the worst sufferer under the system because he was forced into "direct competition with stolen wares." See below, Lttrs. 138–143.

102 ❖ W. M. Rossetti to George Grove

56 Euston Sq. N.W.
22 May /75

My dear Sir,

A very old & valued friend of mine, W. B. Scott has recently (as you may probably be aware) brought out a vol. of Poems,—some of his older ones republished & others new.[1] (A notice of the vol. appears in to-day's Academy—also lately in the Examiner[2]). I shd. like to write something about it somewhere, & wd. gladly do so in Macmillan's Magazine if you think fit. As I feel that a regular review of the book, simply as a new vol. of Poems, wd. not be quite the thing for the Magazine, I shd. propose to take a wider scope, & say something about the developments of English poetry within the period— say 40 years past—that Scott has been writing. If you consent, I wd. set about the article as soon as convenient: but it wd. not be ready for some little while, as I have a deal of other writing on hand.

With best regards, believe me, Dear Sir,
Very truly yours,
W. M. Rossetti

Geo. Grove Esq:

My object is to write the article, whether paid for or not.

At the same time, I presume that, if admitted, it wd. be paid for at the current rate.

———

[1] William says the article was inspired by his desire "to promote the repute of my old friend" (*Remin.*, II, 497). William Bell Scott (1811–1892) met the Rossettis in the winter of 1847–1848 and remained their close friend throughout his lifetime; and therefore posthumous publication of his *Autobiographical Notes,* 2 vols. (1892), attacking DGR, came as a disagreeable surprise to CGR and WMR (see *Christina Rossetti* and *TLS,* June 26, 1959, p. 389). Scott's 1875 *Poems,* illustrated by his etchings and those of Alma Tadema, contained the much-discussed dedicatory sonnet to Swinburne, Rossetti, and Morris.

[2] The *Examiner* was edited between 1874 and 1878 by William Minto (1845–1893), Scott's friend and later the editor of his *Notes* (see above). Consequently the columns of this paper were open to Scott and his friends.

103 ❖ *W. M. Rossetti to George Grove*

56 Euston Sq., N.W.

3 June /75

Dear Mr. Grove,

I am much obliged for your letter authorizing me to send in the article I had proposed about W. B. Scott's poems. The "right of remonstrance" wh. you reserve will I trust not need to be exercised: if I thought it would need, I cd. not but hesitate to write the article at all. For I apprehend that numerous writers known in their respective subjects must send in signed articles (mine wd. be signed) to the Magazine, & <without> get them published, without its being prescribed that their opinions shd. conform in detail to the editorial opinions; &, were a different rule applied to me, this wd. seemingly be on the ground that my opinions are outrageous, or are expressed outrageously—of neither of which defects am I conscious. However, I shall write the article without misgiving as to the result, & send it in, & leave it to its fate.

With thanks & best regards

Very truly yours,

W. M. Rossetti

104 ❖ *Christina Rossetti to*
[*? Routledge Brothers*] [1]

Text: Univ. Texas MS.

56 Euston Square—N.W.

10 June 1875.

Dear Sir

Last night I received the enclosed letter, to which (according to my established custom in such cases) I decidedly wish to say "yes": but I will not return my answer to Mr. Schlesinger [2] without first consulting you. I even think that to have attention thus attracted to Sing Song, in the event of publication of the music, might prove of some advantage to our joint interests. I dare say you will oblige me by returning Mr. Schlesinger's note; and still more by answering me without needless delay, as my reply to him waits on yours to me.

The last I heard of the sale of Sing Song, was when I wrote to you joining you in authorizing a "trade sale" of such copies as [hung] on hand. But since then, wanting a copy, I was surprised to find the price unreduced: and this, together with a report that the little book is procurable at (at least one, if not more) railway stations, has suggested to me a hope that after all some degree of success beyond what at first appeared is attending it. Is it so? The question is of course an interesting one to me, as well as to you: and I do think you and Mr. Hughes helped to make Sing Song so attractive that it fully deserved recognition.

Very sincerely yours

Christina G. Rossetti

---

[1] Although this letter, part of the Charles Fairfax Murray collection purchased by the University of Texas at Sotheby's in 1961, is marked "1 ALS to C. F. Murray," I consider the firm of Routledge Brothers as the more likely recipient. Murray had nothing to do with the "attractiveness" of *Sing-Song* after the F. S. Ellis fiasco in 1870: Hughes was the sole illustrator of the published book. Furthermore, Christina would hardly have consulted Murray about price and permissions.

[2] I do not identify him though I suspect he was either a composer or music publisher.

56 Euston Sq. N.W.
Tuesday 16. [1875] [1]

Dear Mr. Macmillan

Here, at last, is my book. One little piece "Amor Mundi" came out in 1865 (if I recollect rightly) in the Shilling Magazine: how about asking leave to reprint it? [2] I do not recollect any other points questionable.

Very sincerely yours
Christina G. Rossetti

---

[1] Year date by firm for this letter and the following sequence, Lttrs. 106–109.

[2] *Amor Mundi* (*Works*, p. 374) appeared in the May, 1865, issue of *Shilling Magazine*, p. 93, with an illustration by Frederick Sandys (1829–1904), painter and illustrator.

106 ❖ *Christina Rossetti to Alexander Macmillan*

2 Royal Park
Clifton—Bristol
Tuesday 24th [1875]

My dear Mr. Macmillan

This morning 4 proofs suddenly came to hand,—so by some oversight they must have got delayed in Euston Square, & I hope this has not inconvenienced you. If one is ready before the end of this week, please send it me straight here: [1] if not, on the 31st I expect to be at home again.

I have substituted a short new thing for a correspondingly short old thing; & I think the volume rather gains by this: pray think so too. These remarks apply to the proofs I post up to you with this.

Very sincerely yours
Christina G. Rossetti

One of your name, but I know not whether your son or nephew,[2] sent me the obliging assurance whilst you were away that my proofs should go straight to Boston from your office. This I trust meets with your approval, & I owe thanks both to you & your namesake.

---

[1] She was visiting Maria at the All Saints' Mission Home in Clifton, near Bristol. Although she found Clifton a trifle too "Cheltenhamy" for her taste, she enjoyed the Bristol Zoo and the occasional society of Dora Greenwell, the poet, who lived in the vicinity.

[2] Probably AM's son George Macmillan who, according to his own statement, came into the firm in 1874 (*Macm. Lttrs.*, Glasgow ed., p. xliv) though James Foster, compiler of the *Macm. Bib. Cat.*, asserts George did not enter the firm until 1879 (p. vi). AM's nephew, his brother Daniel's eldest son, Frederick Macmillan, later head of the firm, entered the business in 1876, according to George Macmillan (p. xliv) and 1879, according to Foster (p. vi).

107 ❖ *Christina Rossetti to Alexander Macmillan*

2 Royal Park
Clifton.
27 August. [1875]

Dear Mr. Macmillan

Your visit will always be a favour,—mine to your office (where I have never yet been) looks a little formidable. Pending either event, I feel inclined to write my notions on our joint subject of interest.

The illustrations are, I fear, somewhat difficult to manage. Would it be possible to do without any frontispiece or vignette —titlepage, & print off the 4 woodcuts (all alike without text, beyond the quoted line of verse) as in fact 4 plates, each to be inserted opposite the incident it represents? This suggestion rather takes my own fancy, but it may not yours. Another plan proposed to me would be to combine the 2 titlepage cuts into one frontispiece by putting them on top of the other:—

<table>
<tr><td>G.M.
cut</td></tr>
<tr><td>P.P.
cut</td></tr>
</table>

& then to insert the remaining 2 designs each in its proper place. The only plan I feel as inadmissible is to dispense with any one of the 4: but in all else I will be amenable to reason.[1] In the binding I am compliance itself; tho' I shall be pleased if you select the old blocks, one or both, with a widened back to suit increased bulk, if, in so compendious an ed. the bulk be increased. And may I exclude magenta, dense blue (I know not its proper name, but it is like modern laundry blue), & vermillion, as my colours?

Thank you & Mr. George Macmillan for all obliging help. I may not be fixed at home immediately on my return next Tuesday, but may perhaps be going away again awhile. I am not certain. If so, I will recollect & send my address for proofs.

Very truly yours,
Christina G. Rossetti

I fear the "formidableness" of your office may rather seem to you laziness in myself: but pray wink at so subtle a distinction.

---

[1] AM carried out CGR's suggestion to insert the illustrations so that each faced the incident it represented. The first of the four woodcuts, "Buy from us with a golden curl," was, however, used as a frontispiece opposite the title page. The color finally selected for the cover was a cocoa brown (probably darker originally than it is now) with the same design as the 1862 *Goblin Market,* gold lines with three small circles at the corners.

108 ◈ *Christina Rossetti to Alexander Macmillan*

56 Euston Sq. N.W.
Saturday morning. [1875]

Dear Mr. Macmillan

The sheets came safely to hand, & I am getting on with fusion, etc.; but I notice a few poems (e.g. "Sister Maude" [1]) I do not want to reprint at all, & I am anxious to do all thoroughly now I am about it; so I may be a few days longer even now before sending the whole back to you.

I fear the "Germ"[2] has already contributed what it had to contribute, curious old book that it is.

Very sincerely yours

Christina G. Rossetti

---

[1] *Sister Maude* (*Works*, p. 348), written in 1860, a year after *Goblin Market* (March, 1859), deals with the same theme, the "saving" of one sister by another, but in terms which appear to be almost a travesty upon the *Goblin Market* situation. Possibly Christina wished to omit this poem from the new complete edition because of its personal reference to Maria (see my article, *PMLA*).

[2] *The Germ* (1850), the famous but short-lived Pre-Raphaelite periodical, collapsed after four numbers. The January issue contained Christina's *Dreamland* and *An End*, the February issue her *A Pause of Thought* (the first poem of the *Three Stages* series), *O Roses for the Flush of Youth*, and *A Testimony*, and the March number her *Repining* and *Sweet Death* (*Works*, pp. 292, 288, 119, 9, 116).

109 ❖ *Christina Rossetti to Alexander Macmillan*

12 Bloomsbury Sq. W.C.[1]

Tuesday morning. [1875]

Dear Mr. Macmillan

I send you my titlepage. I thought of bringing it round myself this morning, when I remembered an engagement which will have to be kept later on in the day & which will be exertion enough for one day.—I hope I have not been over-careless in not asking for revises of various proofs,—but I dare say it will not signify much.

Very sincerely yours

Christina G. Rossetti

I suppose one more proof may finish off my book!

---

[1] The residence of Christina's maternal aunts, Charlotte and Eliza Polidori.

56 Euston Sq. N.W.
12 Septr. /75.

Dear Mr. Grove,

Here is the article wh. I had proposed to write about the poems of W. B. Scott, associated with the course of our poetry for the last half-century, & wh. you consented to receive by letter dated 28 May.[1] You said the article shd. not exceed 10 pages. I think 10 pages wd. be just about 1000 lines of my handwriting, & have from the first written with that limitation strictly in view: am afraid however that I must have a little exceeded the 10 pages—reaching probably to 11, or maybe 12. I trust you may not particularly object to this.

Believe me
Very faithfully yours,
W. M. Rossetti

Of course I shd. be glad to see a proof.

---

[1] W. M. Rossetti, "William Bell Scott and Modern British Poetry," *Macmillan's Magazine* (March, 1876), 418–429.

111 ❖ *Alexander Macmillan to Miss Ellice Hopkins* [1]

Text: Macm. Lttrs., Glasgow ed., pp. 286–287 (reproduced in part below).

Nov. 29, 1875

. . . What you say of Miss Rossetti is most true. She is very subjective. But so fine, I think. Every word tells enough and no more. I once told her that all her poems were so sad, and she said she did not wonder I felt it so. I have only seen her two or three times and she was very bright and interesting, but she is very delicate in health. She is a true artist and will live.

---

[1] I do not identify her.

56 Euston Square—N.W.—
Saturday evening. [1875] [1]

Dear Mr. Macmillan

I enclose (& do not care to have back) a note which I know not exactly how to answer,—which I have answered, that is, provisionally, referring the decision to you. I dare say you may not think it worth while to send Mr. Ingram [2] a copy, tho' I suppose reviews are to be desired & I own to liking friendly ones.

Having seen my parcel, let me thank you for your kindness in recollecting my wish for an unbound copy.

Very sincerely yours
Christina G. Rossetti

Thank you too for a Glasgow News [3] received.

---

[1] Year date by firm.

[2] John H. Ingram (1849–1916), biographer of Poe, Marlowe, and Oliver Madox Brown, William's brother-in-law, and editor of the *Eminent Women* series (see above, Lttr. 6, n. 1), also used the pseudonym, "Don Felix de Salamanca." Toward the end of November Christina wrote Gabriel, "Do you recollect our being unable to identify a certain 'Don Felix de Salamanca' who published my fac-simile in a No. of the Pictorial World? He turns out to be a certain Mr. Ingram from whom I have heard once or twice, and who would now like to send a notice of my fresh edition to the same periodical: I have referred the matter to Mr. Macmillan for decision" (*Fam. Lttrs.,* pp. 53–54).

[3] In the letter quoted above she said she had "one favorable review of my new edition in *The Glasgow News:* I know of no other, at least yet." On March 25 James Thomson, writing under the initials B.V., reviewed the volume in *The Secularist*. Swinburne, who thought the review "very good," was curious about B.V.'s identity.

56 Euston Square—
Tuesday 7th [December, 1875][1]

Dear Mr. Macmillan

I hope you will agree with me in liking to secure a friendly review in the "Hour"[2] on the terms proposed, & will oblige me by forwarding (if as yet unsent) my volume to the office. I see more stir is excited by my new ed. than I anticipated: I fully believe I have a capital prospect of an article in the Academy,[3] & I understand I am assigned by the Examiner.[4] So I look back with some regret to Mr. Ingram's offered review in the Pictorial World,[5]—regret, that is, if he has not obtained his copy,—& would even now ask you, if I may, to let him have one. Mr. Hake, whose letter please don't return, is a son of Dr. Hake,[6] & himself a rising man in light literature if he carries out his present promise: he has, too, scientific knowledge, & perhaps will enter that field some day & make us all hear of him again.

Very truly yours
Christina G. Rossetti

---

[1] Month and year added by firm.

[2] *The Hour* (1873–1876) was edited by Thomas Hamber.

[3] *The Academy* was started in 1869 by Dr. Charles Appleton (1841–1879), and from 1874 to 1878 William was its art critic. His brother-in-law Francis Hueffer (see below, Lttr. 154 and n. 1) was assistant editor in 1871. Both this periodical and *The Athenæum* announced the forthcoming publication of the volume, *The Academy* (Feb. 27), p. 214, and *The Ath.* (Aug. 21), p. 247.

[4] Scott's friend, W. Minto (see above, Lttr. 102, n. 2), would have seen to it that she was well treated in the *Examiner*. When Watts offered to review the book for that journal, he was told by DGR that she was "safe in the hands of Gosse."

[5] *The Pictorial World* (1874–1892) was edited by H. W. Cutts.

[6] Thomas Gordon Hake (1809–1895), poet and physician, saved Gabriel's life in 1872 when he took an overdose of laudanum. Dr. Hake is remembered today for his *Memoir of Eighty Years* (1892). George Hake, his son and DGR's secretary from 1872 to 1877, wrote the *Hour* review CGR mentions at the beginning of her letter.

During these years occurred the second crisis in Christina's business relations with Macmillan, this time complicated by the fact that she was preparing a third volume of verse for publication. Apparently without consulting her, Macmillan had been applying the proceeds from the 1875 *Goblin Market* to make up the deficit on the 1866 *Prince's Progress*. Once again her brothers thought it necessary to take a hand in her business affairs, and they asked Theodore Watts (Dunton), by profession a solicitor, to represent her in negotiations with Macmillan. She agreed, provided it was strictly understood that the discussion should be on the friendliest possible basis and that she had no intention whatsoever of starting legal proceedings.

Next in interest is the Rossetti-Quilter controversy, which enlivened a few issues of the *Magazine* in 1880. William challenged Harry Quilter, author of the article appearing in the September number called, "The New Renaissance; or the Gospel of Intensity," to produce evidence to support his attack upon William's integrity as a critic. Quilter defended his position in a letter to the editor, but some years later apologized when he needed William's copyright permission to include reproductions of Gabriel's paintings in his *Preferences in Art, Life, and Literature* (1892).

Finally, Christina's letters relating to the publication of *A Pageant and other Poems* (1881), which show her concern about retaining copyright, are of particular interest in view of the fact that the inequity of copyright law was a subject agitating literary and publishing circles in England and America during the 'seventies and 'eighties. Macmillan, a strong advocate of reform, urged his views both in the *Magazine* and as a witness in the parliamentary debate following the report of the Copyright Commission of 1876.

114 ❖ *Christina Rossetti to Alexander Macmillan*

30 Torrington Square—W.C.
4th November 1876.

Dear Mr. Macmillan

Will you oblige me by noting my permanent change of address (see above), & if you please erasing my old address.[1] I wrote formally to your firm announcing the change a month ago; but I fear ineffectually as the November Mag. came as usual to Euston Square. Tho' I must not count on the continuance of a kindness for which I take this opportunity of again thanking you, I yet think it may be convenient on both sides for you to know where I am & where I am not.

However, what I am writing about is not really all that.— I have by me a completed work, a sort of devotional reading-book for the red-letter Saints' Days,[2] which is of course longing to see the light & which I shall be glad if you will consent to look at. It will make a goodish sized volume, if it gets into print. It is, as I say, completed; only I shall add a dedication to my Sister; & if you <u>were</u> to say yes, I should endeavour to obtain for it the revision and sanction of my most kind friend the Rev. H. W. Burrows who did me so great a favour by endorsing "Annus Domini."[3] My M.S. is entitled "Young Plants & Polished Corners," a name connected with the particular plan of the little work;[4] a plan, so far as I know, not as yet hacknied.

I hardly perhaps need ask you not to keep my M.S. long in

suspense if you do not at last adopt it, as I always find you friendly and accessible.

Very sincerely yours

Christina G. Rossetti

---

[1] After William's marriage to Lucy Brown in 1874 (see above, Lttrs. 64, n. 3, and 92, n. 2), he took her to live with his family at Euston Square, but it was not long before "the harmony in the household was not unflawed, and sometimes jarringly interrupted" (*Remin.*, II, 422). The unsatisfactory domestic arrangements continued for two years after what Maria described as "Lucy's enthronement as bride," but in July, 1876, Christina announced to Gabriel that "our Euston Square home-party is broken up," and that she and her mother intended to take a house at Torrington Square with her two aunts, Charlotte and Eliza. On August 22 Mrs. Rossetti wrote Gabriel that she and Christina would move after Michaelmas (Bod. Ross. MS. 22). See also *Christina Rossetti*, pp. 301–303, 311.

[2] *Called to Be Saints*, published 1881 by the Society for the Propagation of Christian Knowledge, which also brought out CGR's other devotional prose works. When Gabriel protested at such particularly committed publication, she made the oft-quoted remark, "I don't think harm will accrue to me from my SPCK books, even to my standing: if it did, I should still be glad to throw my grain of dust into the religious scale" (*Fam. Lettrs.*, p. 92).

[3] CGR's first volume of devotional prose, published by James Parker and Co. (1874). Henry William Burrows (1816–1892) was vicar of Christ Church, Albany Street, from 1851 to 1878, after which he was Canon of Rochester. Christina and he became friends during her twenty years of regular attendance at Christ Church.

[4] The plan of organization consists of sections, each of which contains quotations from Scripture relating to the particular saint under discussion, a short biography of the saint, a prayer and a "memorial," and a brief essay on the flower or gem attributed to the saint. Occasionally an original poem concludes the section.

115 ❖ *Christina Rossetti to* [?]

Text: Univ. Texas MS.

30 Torrington Sq. London—W.C.

6 July. [After 1876]¹

Dear Sir

Pray do not apologize for making an enquiry which it gives me pleasure to answer.

The separate editions of "Goblin Market" and "Prince's Progress" have been out of print for some years past: but both are included (and cannot now be procured singly) in the volume of my collected "Poems" published by Messrs. Macmillan. This volume contains nearly the whole contents of the former ones, with some additional but not principal pieces.

Very sincerely yours

Christina G. Rossetti.

---

¹ Dating mine. The letter could not have been written earlier than 1877, for the move to Torrington Square was not made until the autumn of 1876. See preceding letter (114) and note 1.

116 ❖ *Christina Rossetti to Alexander Macmillan*

30 Torrington Square—W.C.

12th December 1877.

Dear Mr. Macmillan

I have been asked more than once how my last edition had fared, & I never know. Perhaps now that it has been out these 2 years I may venture to enquire whether it has had any degree of sale, or whether it has suffered under the general trade depression & failed.

In the month of Xmas I will anticipate a little & wish you & yours a happy Xmas.

Sincerely yours

Christina G. Rossetti

117 ❖ *Christina Rossetti to Alexander Macmillan*

30 Torrington Sq. W.C.
Wednesday, [December, 1877] [1]

Dear Mr. Macmillan

Thank you for my acceptable little cheque: I dare say our last ed. will begin paying some day. Please let me have, whenever it suits your convenience, my 3 "Goblin Markets"; as I am glad the remnant of that issue should be withdrawn, & you I see take the same view.

I am not very robust, nor do I expect to become so; but I am well content with the privileges & immunities which attach to semi-invalidism.[2] Thank you none the less for wishing me well.

Very sincerely yours
Christina G. Rossetti

---

[1] Marginal note by the firm: "3 sent 19/12/77."

[2] Although William has told us that "any one who did not understand that Christina was an almost constant and often a sadly-smitten invalid, seeing at times the countenance of Death very close to her own, would form an extremely incorrect notion of her corporal, and thus in some sense of her spiritual condition" ("Memoir" to the *Works*, p. 1); my own view is that her numerous illnesses were psychosomatic in origin. She early found semi-invalidism, with its freedom from economic and social responsibilities, congenial to a life in which the production of poetry was paramount.

118 ❖ *Christina Rossetti to Alexander Macmillan*

30 Torrington Square—W.C.
26th April 1878

Dear Mr. Macmillan

I am a little puzzled by the bill I re-enclose, tho' quite happy to pay it at once if that is the correct course. What puzzles me is that (on a former ed.) you once returned me the price, less postage, of a copy for which I forwarded payment. Perhaps however the system now is different? If so, I of course see that my volume will produce profits all the sooner, & that contingency pleases me. The favour I ask is that you will clear my mind, & then I shall know for the future as well as the present what to do. If you say "pay," I will do so by P.O.O. made out to your Firm from my customary signature.

I know however very well indeed that I am indefinitely deep in your debt for unnumbered postages of American letters & other matters extraneous to our business relations: & I ask you to allow me to "lump" some of my obligations in the shape of the enclosed stamps. I think I sent postage for the Burcham copy.[1]

Spring is making even London beautiful: how beautiful the country must be!

Always truly yours
Christina G. Rossetti

---

[1] During the year (1853-1854) Christina and her parents spent in Frome-Selwood, Somerset, William and Maria took bachelor's lodgings over the chemist's shop of Robert P. Burcham in Albany Street, Regents' Park. As an amateur water-color artist of still-life subjects, Burcham became friendly with William and was soon accepted as a friend on the fringe of the Rossetti circle. He was still calling in 1883.

119 ❖ W. M. Rossetti to The Firm

56 Euston Sq. N.W.
16 Jan. /79.

Dear Sirs,

Some while ago you were good enough to send me an account showing a small sum due to me this month from my book *Fine Art chiefly Contemporary*—also that 10 copies remained on hand on 30 June last. Assuming that some such number of copies is still on hand, I wd. thank you to send 5 of them to the above address so that I may have a few copies to meet any request from private friends, after the general stock shall have been exhausted.

I am afraid your experience with this book has not been such as to induce you to look with any favour upon the idea of publishing in a companion volume a selection from my later writings in periodicals, etc. Were there any inclination that way, however, I cd. easily get together such a volume, & shd. of course be well pleased to do so.

Yours very truly,

W. M. Rossetti

Messrs. Macmillan & Co.

120 ❖ *W. M. Rossetti to Alexander Macmillan*

56 Euston Sq. N.W.

24 Jan. [1879] [1]

Dear Macmillan

Thanks for your friendly letter, to wh. I will reply in more detail soon, or will call. Have of late been bothered with gout,[2] & very little out of the house since 21 Decr.—Receipt enclosed.

Yours truly,

W. M. Rossetti

---

[1] Year date by firm.

[2] On January 1 CGR wrote DGR, "Yesterday also William, going out for the first time, came here—looking quite as well as can be expected, but of course pulled down. He was in one large gouty shoe, and was still taking colchicum" (Bell, pp. 72–73).

121 ❖ *Christina Rossetti to The Firm*

30 Torrington Square—W.C.

Saturday, 23 August [1879] [1]

Miss Rossetti presents her compliments to the Firm, & begs that the enclosed may be returned to her without delay, should Mr. Macmillan's absence on the continent, or should any other cause, prevent its reaching him quickly. If possible, however, she greatly wishes him to receive it at once.

―――――――
[1] Year date by firm. The Macmillan stamp at the bottom signifies the letter was received August 25, 1879.

122 ❖ *Christina Rossetti to D. G. Rossetti*
Text: *Fam. Lttrs.*, p. 83 (reproduced in part below).

30 Torrington Square, W.C.
17 December 1879

My Dear Gabriel,

I certainly have two very brotherly brothers who command my affectionate gratitude by their unfailing care for my small concerns. Mr. Watts moreover makes me his debtor by such friendly good will. If he and you and William all agree as to the necessity of the step, and if he will kindly take it without my involving myself in heavy law-expenses, I will accept your opinion that it is advisable and be glad that he should speak to Mr. Macmillan. But only and absolutely in the most amicable manner; as being quite certain that no wrong has either been done or dreamt of, as knowing that I am satisfied with actual arrangements, and as bearing in mind that I stick to my position of cordial personal friendship with my friendly publisher. All which premised, I should of course be glad to have business-matters put—if they are not so already—on a business-footing. Nothing however, not proof positive that I had been pillaged! would make me have recourse to law: this is a statement at once preliminary and final. Moreover I am hugging hopes of getting together before long enough verse for a small fresh volume: so least of all at this moment am I in the mood to alienate the staunch Mac . . .

123 ❖ *Christina Rossetti to D. G. Rossetti*
Text: British Museum MS.

30 Torrington Square—W.C.

26th December 1879

My Dear Gabriel

Thank you for sweet-tooth dainties and an intellectual 'Shadow'.[1] For this latter I have written promptly to Mr. [?] Dobell, on the 'spec' that it may still be attainable.—I hope Mr. Davies [2] will not brand me as rude for not acknowledging the choice card I so much like: but I dare say he will not be at all disturbed!

It seems less formidable to write to you than straight to Mr. Watts, whose good will has my warm thanks.[3] So far as I recollect the 'Goblin Market' business stands thus (N.B. Whenever I talk of 'I said' you must understand 'I wrote': for I have not met Mac for years.)—When the last unstereotyped edition of Goblin Market was within about half a dozen copies of exhaustion, Mr. Macmillan wrote to me proposing a new edition. I said yes. 'Prince's Progress, Etc.', long out of print, were to be included. I carefully wrote out in my letter a statement of our old original terms (his the whole expense and risk: and any profits to be halved between us), and begged him to let me have a written answer accepting definitely these terms. No answer whatever did I receive: but proofs came, and I dropped the subject of terms. When statement of sale began coming in, I perceived that the fresh ed. was paying off the old debt on 'Prince's Progress': well and good. In time this debt was paid off, and at last a little money came in. In the course of this summer a friend wanting a copy of my vol. was informed that there were no copies at the moment but that there soon would be some. After a period of ignorance on my part what this meant, I found out (by a sort of chance in our correspondence) from Mr. Macmillan that more copies could and would shortly be issued, because the last ed. had been stereotyped: without my being consulted; yet doubtless on the supposition that I should <be pleased> consent, as <I am> of course I should.

This is the whole story; and evidently the re-issue is now on sale, because I know of a copy recently bought.

Mamma and Aunt Charlotte got home quite prosperously last night, and with Aunt Eliza send love; Aunt Eliza adding private and personal thanks for the almonds and raisins.

Always affectionately your sister
Christina G. Rossetti

---

[1] Maria's *Shadow of Dante*. Christina may have written to Bertram Dobell, the bookseller.

[2] William Davies (1830–1896), minor poet, painter, and etcher, chiefly remembered for his correspondence with Gabriel. Bell prints a letter from Christina conjecturally dated 1879 in which she tells Gabriel she has just received an endorsed etching by Davies, and asks for his address so that she may "thankfully acknowledge it" (p. 75).

[3] Bell erroneously dates as *circa* 1880 a letter written shortly before Christmas in what must have been the year 1879, for in it CGR thanks DGR "for unfailing brotherliness negociating [*sic*] between Mr. Watts and me. And truly grateful am I to him, whether or not any act ensues; the friendly good-will commands my thanks in either case" (p. 77).

124 ❖ *W. M. Rossetti to George Grove*

5 Endsleigh Gardens.[1]
N.W.
10 Septr. 1880.

Dear Mr. Grove,

I believe you are still the Editor of Macmillan's Magazine:[2] if not, this note is addressed to the Editor, whoever he may be.

Mr. Quilter's article[3] contains a great deal of matter wh. I shd. suppose to be distasteful to the parties concerned, & open to confutation: with this however I have nothing to do. I am myself mentioned only twice, & in each instance I consider the mention to be invidious, & (seemingly) even unfair or incorrect. I always object to seeing in print a wrong statement of _fact_ concerning myself, while as to critical opinion of my performances I take the good & the bad with equal placidity.

My own opinion is that the enclosed remarks of mine ought in fairness to be printed in the magazine, along with any answer wh. Mr. Q. may furnish thereto. If you think otherwise, this will of course not be done: but I shd. like Mr. Q. to see my remarks, & shd. suppose that he will not neglect to send me a reply to them.

With best regards believe me, Dear Mr. Grove,

Very truly yours

W. M. Rossetti

George Grove Esq.

---

[1] About 1878 the south side of Euston Square was renamed Endsleigh Gardens. WMR denies it was because of the shocking "Euston Square murder," and cites a number of subsequent murders in the neighborhood which failed to disturb the residents' equanimity.

[2] He was.

[3] Harry Quilter, "The New Renaissance; or the Gospel of Intensity," _Macmillan's Magazine_ (Sept., 1880), pp. 391–400. Quilter's purpose in writing the article was to attack the new Aestheticism, which, he charged, had started as an esoteric movement within a select coterie of poets, painters, and critics in the mid-'sixties, and had by the beginning of the 'eighties become popular and highly fashionable in all sections of middle class society. His attack was twofold: he censured the new movement on moral grounds and he complained of its monopoly of the arts. He named the Rossetti brothers, Swinburne, Morris, Pater, and Burne-Jones as the leaders of the school. See my forthcoming article, " 'The Gospel of Intensity': William Rossetti and the Quilter Controversy," _Victorian Studies._

125 ❧ _W. M. Rossetti to George Grove_

5 Endsleigh Gardens.

N.W.

20 Septr. /80.

Dear Mr. Grove,

It does appear to me desirable that my note shd. be printed in the Magazine along with Mr. Quilter's reply to it.[1] Your readers have been informed by Mr. Q. that I was in the habit of criticizing my brother's pictures & poems, & I shd. like them to know what amount of credit they are to attach to that one among Mr. Q's various derogatory statements.

As to your suggestion of a general counter-statement from one of the persons chiefly concerned—such as Swinburne, Morris, or my brother—I can only say that I have not as yet had any communication whatever with any one of these persons on the subject: don't know whether any of them have read the article, or how they take it. My own concern was simply to repel mis-statement or unfounded insinuation concerning myself, & I shd. not wish to put myself forward as intermediary with any one else—certainly not with my brother, nor yet with Morris. As to Swinburne, it so happens that I shall be seeing him on Friday, & if the conversation shd. lead to it, I wd. not mind putting him in possession of your views— but this wd. depend on chances of the moment. Mr. Quilter may perhaps be a much more eminent personage in the world of letters than I have at present any idea of—his name not having been known to me (I think) until I saw it appended to the Macmillan article; [2] but as yet my impression is that Swinburne might hardly consider him a foeman worthy of his steel. [3] This may all be my ignorance.

With best regards
Yours very truly,
W. M. Rossetti

---

[1] Grove printed both William's letter and Quilter's reply in the November issue (see below, Lttrs. 126–127).

[2] Best remembered today for *Preferences in Art, Life, and Literature* (1892), Harry Quilter (1851–1907) was then an aspiring young man of letters whose fledgling reputation rested on his biography of Giotto in *The Illustrated Biographies of Great Artists* series (1879). Author of *Sententiae Artis* (1886) and editor of *Is Marriage a Failure?* (1888), he edited the short-lived *Universal Review* from 1888 to 1890. In the 'nineties he became reconciled to William, but Whistler, whose savage ire he aroused upon another occasion, remained his implacable enemy to the end.

[3] In a letter to Watts Swinburne carefully distinguished between

those "foemen worthy of his steel" and "the men of New Grub Street" whose attacks he considered beneath his notice. He had, he said, no intention of ignoring or escaping "the buzz . . . and sting of the vermin of letters in London," but he looked upon it as "a waste of time and temper" and consequent loss of self-respect to keep on the alert "for every passing impertinence that the sons of Curll [Pope's *The Dunciad*] . . . may indulge in, and of which I naturally never should or need hear unless it actually calls for notice as the only alternative to submission . . ." (Lang, III, 177–179).

126 ⬦ *W. M. Rossetti to The Editor*

Text: Macmillan MS. Published: *Macmillan's Magazine* (November, 1880), p. 80.

DEAR SIR

In an article written by Mr. Harry Quilter in *Macmillan's Magazine* for September, named *The New Renaissance,* I find two sentences relating to myself. The first is this: "The temptation of course was very great for Mr. W. M. Rossetti to write complimentary criticism of Mr. Swinburne." The second sentence is this: "We know that . . . one Rossetti wrote poems and painted pictures, and the other wrote criticism on them, and so influenced both arts."

Some sort of imputation upon me appears to be intended in these sentences, taken in their general context.

I should like to learn from Mr. Quilter what is the reason why (in his opinion) the temptation was very great for me to write complimentary criticism of Mr. Swinburne, and why this should be "of course." Also whether his second sentence means (as, according to grammatical rules, it naturally would mean) that I wrote criticisms on the poems and pictures of my brother Dante Rossetti; if so, what is the evidence which he adduces in proof of this. If he merely means that I wrote criticism on poems and pictures (other than those of my brother), I must be excused for expressing a wish that the laxity of his diction had been exercised upon some topic not involving my character for critical probity.

W. M. Rossetti

Text: *Macmillan's Magazine* (Nov., 1880), p. 80.

DEAR SIR,—I regret that Mr. W. M. Rossetti's sensitiveness to criticism should compel me to enter in your pages upon a subject which can hardly be of the slightest interest to any one but Mr. Rossetti himself. Nevertheless, as he has challenged me to explain and justify certain assertions I reluctantly proceed to do both as briefly as possible. As to the first matter mentioned in Mr. Rossetti's letter—if personal friendship, identity of artistic creed, and fellowship in literary work, do not constitute a "great temptation" to favourable criticism, then men are much stronger and surrounding influences much weaker, than I have previously supposed. The 'Of course, etc.' referred to merely meant that the friendship and sympathy were matters of public knowledge.

As to Mr. Rossetti's second question, I need only refer him to the preface of a volume of collected criticisms published by him in 1867 [1] in which he states that he shall not there reprint any of his critical notices on his brother's pictures, not because he fears to reproduce with the authority of his name what had first been written anonymously, but because such criticisms are comparatively slight and unimportant, owing to his brother's best pictures never having been publicly exhibited.

Allow me to say in conclusion that no imputation whatever upon Mr. W. M. Rossetti's "critical probity" was intended by me in the article which has evoked his censure, nor is any imputation intended in this reply, which nothing but Mr. Rossetti's reiterated demand would have elicited, and which, as far as I am concerned, must be considered final.

---

[1] *Fine Art* (1867). See above, Lttr. 61, n. 2. In the preface William explains why he has omitted critical notices of his brother from the volume: neither *"mauvais honte"* nor the fear of being misunderstood would have prevented him from including critical essays about his brother, whose importance in the Pre-Raphaelite school of painting he has no desire to minimize, but "the real and only reason why I do not here republish any reviews of my brother is simply that he never has

been to any moderate extent an exhibiting artist, and that consequently I never have had an opportunity of criticising his works; except in two or three instances, when the works exhibited were of secondary importance, and the reviews were correspondingly slight. As I have thus no adequate notices of my brother's productions to reissue, I prefer not to reissue any at all" (p. xiv).

128 ❖ Christina Rossetti to Alexander Macmillan

30 Torrington Square
W.C.
April 18. 1881.

Dear Mr. Macmillan

I find I have at last enough material for another fresh volume of verse.[1] Will you care to undertake it on the old terms? If so, please oblige me by re-stating those terms in your answer; not that any such formality seems of consequence while you and I live, but because some day an involvement might ensue among those who come after us.[2] I am sure you will kindly answer me at your earliest convenience.

Very sincerely yours
Christina G. Rossetti

---

[1] *A Pageant and Other Poems* (1881).
[2] Although the dispute of 1879 (see Introduction to 1876–1881, and Lttrs. 122, 123) had been settled to the satisfaction of all parties, Christina was running no risk of future misunderstandings.

129 ❖ Christina Rossetti to Alexander Macmillan

30 Torrington Square
W.C.
April 20. 1881

Dear Mr. Macmillan

Thank you for welcoming my offered M.S.,—& I hope & dare say we shall come to one mind.

But copyright is my hobby: with it I cannot part. If it is of any value I think I have the first claim upon it, & if it is of none it may gracefully be left to me! [1]

So, you see, I cannot proceed to sign the proposed Form, either for my old volume or for my new. Please write me back something that may help matters forward. I am, thank you, so wonderfully stronger than I used to be that I could easily call at the Office & talk the business over with you: but I think one often gets on better & keeps more to one's point in a letter.

Always very sincerely yours

Christina G. Rossetti

---

[1] Although Christina "invariably reserved copyright," it would seem that Macmillan was the last man against whom she would need to protect herself. Since 1861 he had been advising his authors not to part with copyright, and in 1873 he published in his magazine Sir John (Lord) Coleridge's article exposing the injustice done Wordsworth. He himself subsequently wrote to Coleridge protesting against the inequities inherent in the Copyright Act of 1842, then in force, which protected an author for only forty-one years during his lifetime and his heirs for only seven years after his death. "Theoretically I have no absolute belief in property at all, and have a sneaking kindness for Communism of the old Platonic or Christian kind. But if we have Property with a big or small p, do, please, let it be on an *equitable* basis. Why the Duke of Bedford should compel me to pay him certain sums of money annually because I have built a nice house on a bit of land which he says is his, and Wordsworth's poems should be open to be made mincemeat of, by me or any publisher who chooses to be reckless in what he does, provided only he does business, I cannot understand. . . . I read some years ago every word I could find written presenting the semblance of a reason for this state of things, and the more I read the more I became convinced that if we are to have property at all, property in literature is that which stands on the soundest basis of public as well as private benefit" (*Macm. Lttrs.,* Glasgow ed., pp. 271–72).

Three years later Macmillan was one of the witnesses called in the parliamentary debate following the report of the Copyright Commission of 1876, and in 1880 he published in his magazine Grant Allen's article (see above, Lttr. 101 and n.) which argued for universal, international copyright, an ideal partly but not altogether realized in our own day.

30 Torrington Square
W.C.
Saturday, April 23, 1881

Dear Mr. Macmillan

Your assurance that I do not lose copyright reconciles me to the Form for both volumes.[1] So please send me such a Form as you propose, either for each edition or for all editions as you like best. I see with satisfaction that you erase the clause about <u>corrections</u>, so trust I may improve my text as often as I please: will it not be so? There remains really nothing to discuss verbally: I hope I worried you less than I worried myself by misunderstanding business terms. My brother's wife has just presented us all with <u>twins</u>![2] so the minutest prospective gains become of double value, & I cling to my dear copyright more than ever—if possible and so to say.

Always truly yours
Christina G. Rossetti

---

[1] Elsewhere Macmillan clarified the terms he was accustomed to offering authors for whose works he could not forecast "a large or immediate popularity." Half-profits, he explained, did not deprive the author of copyright; "they only make us joint holders of it with you." If the firm did not undertake a new edition within six months after the last edition was sold out, the copyright reverted "absolutely" to the author (*Macm. Lttrs.,* Glasgow ed., p. 310). The author he was addressing was J. Henry Shorthouse and the novel for which great popularity could not be predicted was *John Inglesant* (1881). See Morgan, pp. 120–122.

[2] Mary Elizabeth Madox Rossetti (1881–1947) and Michael Ford Madox Rossetti (1881–1883). A few days later Christina wrote William, " 'Io anche—'! At last I took the plunge and sent in some poems to Macmillan, who before he saw accepted them,—for I wrote first on the subject, and he closed with them forthwith. I am somewhat in a quake, a fresh volume being a formidable upset of nerves,—but at any rate, it cannot turn out <u>TWINS</u>!" (*Fam. Lttrs.,* p. 93).

30 Torrington Square
W.C.
April 26. 1881.

Dear Mr. Macmillan

I am much obliged for the Form in duplicate, and shall sign it more than readily. But I forgot in my former letter to ask you what I am to do about Messrs. Roberts of Boston? I feel bound to defer if I can to their wish (should they entertain such a wish) to publish this volume also for the U.S.A. public, but I recollect that <u>you</u> have an American house:[1] I hope you will not object to the offer being made them of the volume, and in that case I dare say you will oblige them and me by furnishing them with early sheets if that is desirable. But how are they to be got at? Shall I write to them or will you?

I trust that this will be our last difficulty; and that then I shall have the pleasure of returning the Form, in company with the M.S. which only waits a finishing look thro' before being delivered over to you.

As to stereotyping I am sure you will do me the favour of judging what is best for our common interest,—but I think it looks grand to be stereotyped!

Very sincerely yours
Christina G. Rossetti

----

[1] Established in 1869, the American branch was in charge of Macmillan's first agent, George Edward Brett. AM's nephew Frederick, later head of the business, spent five years in America looking after the firm's interests there. In the reorganization which in 1896 followed the death of AM and of Brett, the American branch was incorporated as an independent firm, with Brett's son, G. P. Brett, as president.

132 ❖ *Christina Rossetti to Alexander Macmillan*

30 Torrington Square
W.C.
April 27. 1881

Dear Mr. Macmillan

I am quite delighted with our plans and my prospects, and am truly obliged by the ready kindness with which you are serving me.[1] Of course I will, as you suggest, write at once to Messrs. Roberts. I send you the Form signed, retaining the signed duplicate. Also the copy, all ready: perhaps you suspected I was not quite so ready!

Very truly yours
Christina G. Rossetti

------

[1] "I am quite pleased about Macmillan," Christina wrote Gabriel on May 2, "because he said yes without asking to see the M.S. or making a single enquiry as to either bulk or subject. I hope the apparent lag of your proofs is merely because the publishing moment (October?) must now be awaited: perhaps mine may be ready by that date, but about this I know nothing whatsoever. I have not yet, as you may guess, received my first sheet . . ." (*Fam. Lttrs.*, p. 93).

133 ❖ *Christina Rossetti to Alexander Macmillan*

30 Torrington Square
W.C.
Saturday [1881]

Dear Mr. Macmillan

I have got my first proof and hope very soon to send it back. Of course you know best as to bulk,—but I did not know my copy would bear such compendious printing. I computed its prospects by a minute comparison with the pretty old "Goblin Market" edition, and on this basis judged it sufficient for a volume. At any rate I may count (may I not?) on no 2 poems sharing pages or part-pages, and on all sets of sonnets being treated as so many separate sonnets.[1]

137

Please favour me with a reassuring line, and believe me
Very truly yours
Christina G. Rossetti

---

[1] See below, Lttr. 150 and n. 3.

134 ❖ *Christina Rossetti to* [*Charles Fairfax Murray*] [1]

Text: Univ. Texas MSS.

30 Torrington Square—W.C.
June 17. 1881.

Dear Sir

You asked me to let you know if some day I had another "printer's copy" on hand. I have two now. One of a volume of miscellaneous poems to be issued by Macmillan. The second I should not even name to you but for the circumstance of its containing a small number of verse-pieces not elsewhere printed. It is the M.S. of the <u>original</u> (not the <u>compiled</u>) portion of a little book coming out with the S.P.C.K.; and consists partly of prose, partly of verse.[2] It is however a shabby looking copy.

Very sincerely yours
Christina G. Rossetti.

134A ENCLOSURE: *Christina Rossetti to Charles Fairfax Murray*

30 Torrington Sq. London.
23 August 1879

Received of Charles Fairfax Murray Esq. the sum of ten pounds for printers' copy of my forthcoming work "Seek and Find." [3]

Christina G. Rossetti

£10.0.0

[1] Both the envelope addressed to Murray and the enclosed receipt leave no doubt that he was the recipient.

[2] *Called to Be Saints* (1881). See above, Lttr. 114, n. 2.

[3] The receipt, dated 1879, is for *Seek and Find,* published by the S.P.C.K. that year. My guess would be that Murray filed together the 1879 receipt and the 1881 letter, since they both pertained to printers' copies of Christina's publications.

135 ❖ *Christina Rossetti to George Lillie Craik*

Fayremead———Sevenoaks [1]
July 22. [1881]

Dear Mr. Craik

Thank you for an encouraging remark at a formidable moment.[2] Thank you too for enlightening me as to the mysterious "trade subscription." 6/– seems a reasonable price, and I hope I shall be reckoned worth it!

I wonder if I may send you two more names for copies to be sent to, or if I ought formally to write to the Firm? Meanwhile I adopt the lazy course, and if this is too free and easy beg your pardon.

Miss Rintoul [3]
11 Beaumont St.
Portland Place
W.

Mrs. Heimann [4]
20 Brecknock Crescent
Camden Road—N.W.

Hoping that Mr. Macmillan is enjoying a pleasant holiday, and that as pleasant a one awaits Mrs. Craik and yourself,

Very truly yours
Christina G. Rossetti

[1] As usual, Christina managed to be out of town during publication. She spent from July 13 to August 13 at Sevenoaks with her mother and

two aunts, the four sharing the "high" rent of four guineas weekly for Fayremead, which she described as "quite a gentleman's house." Year date added by firm.

[2] Her letters before publication indicate her nervousness about the approaching ordeal. On July 20 she wrote William, "Only think,— my Poems are to come out next Monday. I should have fancied this moment was between 2 publishing seasons, but it seems unlikely that a sane publisher should not understand his business better than I do, and I am not belligerating" [sic]. Publication, however, was delayed, thus increasing her suspense. See *Christina Rossetti*, p. 340.

Watts-Dunton reviewed the volume for *The Athenæum* (Sept. 10), pp. 327–328, and Hall Caine for *The Academy* (Aug. 27), p. 152. Needless to say, both DGR's friends did the handsome thing by his sister.

[3] Henrietta Rintoul, the daughter of the founder and first editor of *The Spectator,* of which William was art critic from 1850 to 1858, was a lifelong friend of Christina's, appearing in her correspondence as early as 1855 and as late as 1888 (see below, Lttr. 153). A frequent caller during 1881–1882, she was one of the women Christina recommended to Ingram as particularly qualified to undertake a biography in his series. She was, said Christina, "an invaluably accurate as well as a practised writer," one, moreover, who moved "in a brilliant circle which her own talents enabled her to adorn" (Troxell, pp. 167, 176–177).

[4] In 1840 Dr. Adolf Heimann, Professor of German at University College, taught the Rossetti children German in exchange for Italian lessons from their father Gabriele Rossetti (1783–1854), then Professor of Italian at King's College. Dr. Heimann married Amelia Barnard in 1843, described as "a very pretty pleasant young English Jewess." Mrs. Heimann, like Miss Rintoul, was one of Christina's oldest and most valued friends.

136 ❖ *Christina Rossetti to Alexander Macmillan*

30 Torrington Square—W.C.
Wednesday night.
Aug. 17th. 1881.

Dear Mr. Macmillan

I hope you will enjoy yourself in Scotland.[1] The little I know of that fine country retains a choice nook in my memory.[2]

Allow me to send 8 dozen postage stamps. I had 6 more copies (my own personal 6), and besides there are chance postages against me for letters you kindly forward to me from time to time, and for which I owe you thanks.

Very sincerely yours

Christina G. Rossetti

---

[1] Macmillan prided himself on being a Scotsman. The family came from Argyleshire, and as he puts it, were "steadfast, God-fearing men." Though his maternal grandfather came from a Lowland Renfrewshire family who had previously settled in Arran, the Macmillans had always lived in the Highlands. Once in questioning an author's use of Scottish words, Macmillan said that as an Ayrshire man, he fancied himself "as belonging to the classic land of Burns, to have an eye and ear for the true Doric" (*Macm. Lttrs.,* Glasgow ed., p. 130). He returned to Scotland frequently for visits, and though he felt thoroughly at home in England and admired English scenery, he confessed to his cousin, an Arran man, that he "could weep with longing after Glen Sannox this very moment, and the great glen over to Lochranza is tender in my memory, like the dear lost friends with whom it is bound up. How I should like a walk with you from Corrie, say, to Lochranza over to the loch and home by the shore. Wouldn't we become poetical!" (*ibid.,* pp. 212–213).

[2] CGR knew Ayrshire well from her visits to Alice Boyd at Penkill Castle near Girvan, Ayrshire. See my *TLS* article (June 26, 1959), p. 389, and *Christina Rossetti,* pp. 215–224, 252–254.

1882–1889

The correspondence during these years is of a more miscellaneous nature than heretofore. One sequence of Christina's letters reveals her efforts to protect her English copyright by securing English publication of a poem before it was published in America. Another consists of references to Macmillan's publication of William Sharp's biography of Gabriel, who died in April, 1882. As Christina's fame increased, she was frequently annoyed by solicitations for aid, financial or professional. She championed some of these causes; and a few of her letters, as well as William's, request Macmillan's assistance for friends or strangers.

137 ❖ W. M. Rossetti to George Lillie Craik

5 Endsleigh Gardens.
N.W.
3 June /82

Dear Mr. Craik,

I am very much obliged for your friendly letter: please excuse a short answer, as I am in a hurry.

I have not the least objection to Mr. Sharp's writing and publishing a book such as he proposes:[1] indeed I don't see that I cd. raise or maintain any objection even if I felt such—wh. however I don't. It might or might not be expedient for me to accept the dedication of the book if offered to me (as seems intended): this is the only point I leave over. Sharp was always a persona grata to my dear brother, & also to myself, & I wish him success.

Very truly yours,
W. M. Rossetti

---

[1] William Sharp (1855-1905), poet, biographer, critic, and man of letters, managed two successful literary careers simultaneously, the second under the name of Fiona McLeod, the nom de plume with which he signed his Celtic romances in prose and verse. He met the Rossettis in 1879 through Sir Noel Patton, and became a warm admirer of both Gabriel and Christina. After Gabriel's death in April, 1882, he wrote *Dante Gabriel Rossetti, a Record and a Study* (1882), described by William as "a rather elaborately planned and very eulogistic book" (*Remin.*, II, 506). See below, Lttr. 139 and n. 1.

30 Torrington Square—W.C.
July 27. 1882.

Dear Mr. Macmillan

Is there a chance of your liking to have a Xmas Carol I have written (9 5-line stanzas) for your January Magazine? I seem indeed asking the question betimes, but somewhere I must endeavour to bring out this Carol which is coming out for Xmas in "Wideawake" (Boston) and of which I want to secure to myself the English copyright. Thro' this circumstance I am on the other hand bound not to get it published here before December 15.

Please favour me with a yes or no, as in default of you I must look elsewhere.

Always sincerely yours
Christina G. Rossetti

30 Torrington Square—W.C.
July 29. 1882.

Dear Mr. Macmillan

Thank you for friendly influence in my favour with Mr. Grove. I must hope that "Wideawake" will not cross the Atlantic before my countermine is in working order: but in no case can I clash with my Boston editor, as the Carol is actually promised.

I need not tell you what an interest we are taking in Mr. Sharp's Memoir.[1] Little did we think that our dear Gabriel would already become the subject of memorials. William has now a wife and 5![2]—no wonder if he is not very sedulous in morning calls.

I will write a word of inquiry as to when to send in the
Carol, straight to Mr. Grove.

Sincerely yours
Christina G. Rossetti

---

[1] On July 26 Christina wrote William, "Mr. Sharp has paid us two
visits, one this afternoon, all about the book . . . Some of the Memoir
of Gabriel I really admire, so I have far from ended at mere laughter
at the style" (*Fam. Lttrs.,* p. 120). Clearly CGR did not entertain a
high opinion of Sharp's literary gifts.

[2] Olivia Frances Madox Rossetti (1875–1960), Gabriel Arthur (1877–
1932), Helen Maria (1879–), and the twins. (See above, Lttr. 130 and
n. 2).

140 ⋄ *Christina Rossetti to* [? *George Grove*]

30 Torrington Square—W.C.
Monday 18. Sept. [1882]

Dear Sir

I have been unusually busy just lately, and this has led me
not at once to avail myself of your permission to show you the
Carol. Now, here it is.[1] I am in hopes you will accept it, but if
you do not like it, pray do not out of kindness hesitate to tell
me so, as between this and January (that no. being the earliest
in which I am at liberty to bring it out) I dare say I can find
some humbler Magazine by aid of which to save my English copyright. Your letter shows me that I may revise the
proof, which I like to do.

Very sincerely yours
Christina G. Rossetti

---

[1] "A Holy Heavenly Chime" (*Works,* p. 279). Published in *Wide-
Awake* (Dec., 1882), pp. 102–103.

141 ❖ Christina Rossetti [to ? George Grove]

30 Torrington Square—W.C.
October 11. 1882.

Dear Sir

I feel very grateful for your kind answer when I have involved everything so vexatiously, and I shall be genuinely disappointed if the only course left open is to withdraw the Carol from Macmillan's Magazine, where I would far rather have had it appear than in Wide Awake. From the latter however it is obviously impossible that I should now secede, as I have been paid for the lines and have posted my receipt. Yet you will see how innocently I have involved matters (if so it be), when I tell you that the date before which I am engaged not to let the Carol appear in England was distinctly stated to me "December 15" and all along I have understood that it is equally to appear in the (so-called) Xmas no. of Wideawake. The only thing I can think of now to do, is to write at once to the Editress Mrs. Ella Farman Pratt [1] and ask her distinctly how the matter stands: at the worst I must put up with my own loss, and very reluctantly with what you obligingly treat as yours. So I will write to Boston, and in due course let you know the result.

Sincerely your obliged
Christina G. Rossetti

---

[1] Ella Farman Pratt (1837–1907) edited *Wide-Awake* from 1875 to 1891, and then co-edited it with her husband, Charles Stuart Pratt, from 1891 to 1893, at which time it was merged with *St. Nicholas*. For a brief history of this publication, see Frank Luther Mott, *The History of American Magazines, 1865–1885,* 4 vols. (New York, 1938), III, 508–509.

142 ✦ *Christina Rossetti to Ella Farman Pratt*
Text: Troxell, pp. 172–173.

30 Torrington Square—London—W.C.
England
October 11. 1882.

DEAR MADAM

Perhaps my last letter (containing my receipt) is already in your hands. If so, you are aware that I have been so fortunate as to get my Xmas Carol into the January "Macmillan." But now I observe printed at the foot of the "Wide Awake" wrapper:—

> "London: James Clarke and Co.
> 13 Fleet Street"—.

I hope this does not indicate that Wide Awake is <u>published in London</u> as well as in Boston: if so, I must in common fairness explain my mistake to Mr. Macmillan's Editor. Indeed, I have already written to him stating what I fear is the case; and he has replied most kindly, setting me free in case of need from any obligation towards him altho' desirous if feasible to retain the Carol. Will you very kindly tell me whether or not any question of copyright forbids simultaneously publication of the Carol by Mr. Lothrop [1] in Boston and by Mr. Macmillan here in London? and also whether Macmillan's Magazine issued on the 22nd or 23rd December will in fact be <u>preceded</u> in the London market by Wide Awake? for if so, it materially alters matters as I imagined them to exist.

Thanking you in anticipation for the reply I look forward to, I remain

Very sincerely yours
CHRISTINA G. ROSSETTI

I am anxious, but am mainly anxious simply to do what is fair to all parties.

---

[1] Daniel Lothrop, the publisher of *Wide-Awake*.

143 ❖ *Christina Rossetti to [?George Grove]*

30 Torrington Square—W.C.
November 3. 1882.

Dear Sir

Last night your forbearing note reached me, and this morning came my fatal enclosure. So I can but accept the kindness with which you refuse to call me to account for my share in this vexatious business.

Will the sonnet [1] I send be of any use either towards refilling the emptied space or occupying a page in some other no.? It will be a real satisfaction to me if in any degree I can make amends.

Gratefully & sincerely yours
Christina G. Rossetti

---

[1] This must have been *A Wintry Sonnet* (*Works,* p. 413), published April, 1883, p. 498, the only poem of CGR's to appear in the *Magazine* that year.

144 ❖ *Christina Rossetti to Alexander Macmillan*

30 Torrington Square—W.C.
January 16. 1883

Dear Mr. Macmillan

May I approach you with what does not even amount to a request?

I do not suppose any Italian work is likely to be included among your many undertakings. Yet as a forlorn hope I venture to tell you of an accomplished Italian gentleman to whom the dear sister and brother I have lost (besides other of us) were substantially helpful.

Dr. Olivieri,[1] whose actual address is 5 Bull Street
Birmingham,
writes to me in a letter received this morning:—

"I am conversant with Italian, French, Latin, English, Spanish, Portuguese and I can translate from and into these languages. In Italian I can write both in poetry and prose. I do not object to any kind of work even copying."

I have not seen Dr. Olivieri, but my sister looked for and found in the Museum Catalogue works he mentioned as being of his own composition. I am convinced that to remain at Birmingham cannot be any object with him: doubtless he would thankfully transfer himself to London if work were found here. His health is delicate and he has a family.

These details I have not verified: but my sister was convinced of his veracity, and we have heard from him at intervals during many years past,—how long ago the first time I know not.

Please, if not too tiresome, let this letter lurk somewhere in case any improbable opening should occur. And thus make me more than ever

Your obliged
Christina G. Rossetti

---

[1] William identifies Agostino Olivieri as "an estimable and cultivated Italian, much afflicted by ill-health and other troubles." On December 23, 1880, Gabriel wrote his mother, "Yesterday I had a note from poor Dr. Olivieri, enclosing a little book of Italian stories for schools, with a dedicatory MS. Sonnet to myself. Poor man! I felt what this must mean at Christmas-time, and responded as best I could. I have no doubt he deserves sympathy. He spoke with much gratitude of your anonymous donation" (*DGRFL*, II, 364–365). Olivieri's works, written during the 'fifties and 'sixties, occupy a respectable space in the British Museum Catalogue.

145 ❖ *Christina Rossetti to F. S. Ellis*
Text: British Museum MS.

30 Torrington Square—W.C.
22 January 1883

Dear Mr. Ellis

I thank you very gratefully for the 5£ which I re-enclose to you. It never occurred to me that you might make such a response to my letter,—it occurred only to your generously kind heart. But the case stands thus. We all implicitly believe in Dr. O. whose serious literary work can be found in the Museum Catalogue (under the name of "Agostino Olivieri"), and on our belief we have acted from time to time. But altho' our acquaintance has subsisted for years, it has been carried on by correspondence,—not one of us has ever seen our interesting friend. He has written to us from various places at home and abroad, but we have never in all these years met. Such being the position of affairs, I cannot feel justified in accepting for him your munificent "loan"—: for whilst I should not hesitate to lavish my own 5£ (if I had them to lavish), I do not feel able to vouch from distinct personal knowledge for all I allege. To ask work for him, I feel fully able: that being quite another affair.[1]

To see what you do with money, makes me the more regret that my unlucky "Commonplace" should have wasted any of yours.

My mother and I are proud and pleased looking at our dear Gabriel's works both at the R.A. and at the Fine Arts Club.[2] I am glad you possess some of those he has left after—after all —not a very prolonged life.

Very truly your obliged

Christina G. Rossetti

---

[1] CGR penned a third appeal to Watts on March 24, explaining that she had written to her publishers "and others all in vain, seeking work for him" (Troxell, pp. 168–169).

[2] The Royal Academy exhibition was promoted by F. R. Leyland, a wealthy Liverpool shipowner and art collector, Rossetti's patron and friend. William found it ironic that "an artist who had been ignored by the Academy throughout his lifetime—and who indeed had ignored the Academy not less decisively—should after his decease be represented on the Academy-walls in an exhibition which the members put together and controlled, and of which they reaped the profit, if any . . ." (*Remin.*, II, 520). He further suspected the Academy officials of purposely hanging his brother's pictures disadvantageously until a protest was published in the *Times*. The second 1883 exhibit at the Burlington Fine Arts Club was arranged by Henry Virtue Tebbs, solicitor and art

collector, who had handled the legal details involved in Gabriel's recovery of his poems from his wife's grave.

146 ❖ *W. M. Rossetti to Alexander Macmillan*

5 Endsleigh Gardens.
N.W.
15 Decr. /84.

Dear Mr. Macmillan;

Mrs. Burton (wife of a painter [1] who has done some works of considerable mark) has asked me whether I cd. give her a few lines of introduction to you; as she is anxious to get some tale or tales of hers published in a magazine, & she naturally thinks of your magazine among the very first. I have not seen the tales wh. Mrs. Burton has at present on hand; but I have seen a tale of hers in Blackwood's Magazine for Septr. last, named *Fiddlers Three*,[2] & have found it bright in invention, touching in sentiment, & written with much grace and facility. I shd. feel pleased & proud if by any aid of mine Mrs. Burton were to succeed in her wish, & obtain a footing in one of your magazines.

With best regards believe me

Always yours truly,
W. M. Rossetti

Alex. Macmillan Esq.

---

[1] This must be William Shakespear Burton (1825–1916), not Sir Frederick W. Burton, Director of the National Gallery, though both men were painters and members of the Rossetti circle. WMR describes the former as "a painter of high aims, and of attainment insufficiently recognized" (*Remin.*, II, 226). In 1866 Gabriel wrote to Howell imploring him to do something about "that poor W. S. Burton," who perennially seemed to be "in the most pitiably destitute state," and who was "really a desperate case" (University of Texas Collection). In one letter Gabriel suggested appealing to Ruskin, who had taken some notice of Burton's picture, "The Wounded Cavalier."

[2] Issue of September, 1884, pp. 363–379. The story deals with three strolling musicians who test out their theories about which kind of music has the greatest popular appeal.

147 ❖ *Christina Rossetti to Alexander Macmillan*

[January, 1885]

Dear Mr. Macmillan

I thankfully return my receipt for your highly satisfactory cheque. With it permit me to transmit 2/6 in stamps for those occasional postages which my "unknown correspondents" inflict on you: I hope you do not translate them all as "curmudgeons"!

Our first transaction in the new year invites me to wish happiness and all blessings to you and yours in 1885.

Always truly yours
Christina G. Rossetti

148 ❖ *Christina Rossetti to The Firm*

30 Torrington Square—W.C.
October 14. 1886.

Dear Sirs

I am quite glad of an opportunity of saying a word for poor Mr. William Bryant,[1] of whose distressed circumstances, impaired health, and ability to work in some departments of literature, I entertain no doubt. It is now some considerable time—perhaps 2 or 3 years—since he first wrote to me, and I then got his statement confirmed by the gentleman to whom he referred me, and who is an acquaintance of my own.

I say I may have known him for 2 or 3 years past, but I am so bad at dates that should the period on comparing notes turn out to be something different, such a discrepancy will not invalidate any other of my beliefs.

Allow me to wish him good friends in your Firm and to remain

Very truly yours
Christina G. Rossetti

---

[1] See below, Lttr. 149 and n.

149 ☙ *Christina Rossetti to William Bryant*

Text: British Museum MS.

Tuesday

29th [?1886/1888]

Dear Mr. Bryant

Perhaps you deprecate my letters as—only in a limited sense —I do yours.

Pray do not go on asking for these petty sums which fritter away my resources for helping you at a future moment. If you will not be firm I must endeavour to become so. When I promised you 3£ it was exclusively with the object of promoting you and your wife's fresh start at Manchester, and was limited to that contingency, which removal I hope might relieve both you and myself. The 3£ are now reduced to £2.10.0; and I am neither willing to sink the sum yet further, nor to replace the deficit. So once more I warn you not to feel disappointed if I decline to read your letters, or to keep us both in the cold holding uncomfortable conversations. I cannot afford to assist you indefinitely, and it is my duty to live within my means. I heartily wish well to your wife and you, but my own ill doing by spending too much cannot be the right way of aiding you. Do not answer, as there is nothing to be answered.[1]

Christina G. Rossetti

---

[1] William Bryant of Clerkenwell was the most unscrupulous of all the beggars who importuned Christina. William tells us that "a certain Mr. B. was for successive years in the habit of writing to Christina . . . for money," and that she, "always more than willing to be charitable to the extent of her modest means, and who lived in permanent dread of failing in one or other item of Christian duty, used in reply to send some small sums enclosed in letters equally redolent of sympathy and of politeness." Thereupon Mr. B. would sell her letters as autographs. A group of nine letters, written by Christina to Bryant between 1886 and 1888, is now in the Yale University Library. For extracts see S. Gorley Putt, "Christina Rossetti, Alms-giver," *English* (Autumn, 1961), pp. 222–223. Possibly the sixteenth letter in the Ellis group of the

British Museum Additional Manuscripts series (41, 130, p. 192), the only one not addressed to Ellis (see above, Lttr. 68, n. 1), may be a stray from the Bryant correspondence. It is headed Friday morning and has "after 1876" inserted in square brackets. The conjectural date, not in Christina's handwriting, is in pencil.

150 ❖ *Christina Rossetti to The Firm*

30 Torrington Square—W.C.
November 24. [1886] [1]

Dear Sirs

I received the little volume (thank you) some days ago; but the letter referring to it only this evening, this latter having gone astray to my brother's house.

As to *Goblin Market* is it possible that Miss Woods [2] wishes to reprint the <u>entire</u> text? If this is indeed her and your wish I consent,—but on no account if any portion whatever is to be omitted. <u>G.M.</u> seems to me bulky, and I observe abridgements (one or more) in the First Reading Book: wherefore it behooves me to forestall any risk of like treatment. I now make a point of refusing extracts, even in the case of my Sonnet of Sonnets some of which would fairly stand alone: [3] so please do not think me disobliging in this particular case.

Very truly yours
Christina G. Rossetti

At the worst surely some of my shorter pieces would do very well, if for any reason I am wanted.

---

[1] Stamped by the firm, "Nov. 25, 1886." Year date written in pencil.

[2] Probably Miss M. A. Woods, Head Mistress of the Clifton High School for Girls, whose *A First School Poetry Book* Macmillan published in 1886 and reprinted with alterations and additions in 1887. The same year the firm brought out her *A Second School Poetry Book*.

[3] In 1883 CGR replied to the editor of an American anthology, who had asked permission to include her poems in his collection, "I do not mind what piece you select, subject only to your taking any piece in question <u>in its entirety</u>; and my wish includes your <u>not</u> choosing an

independent poem which forms part of a series or group,—not (for instance) one no. of 'Passing Away' [the third and last of the *Old and New Year Ditties, Works,* pp. 190–191] or one Sonnet of 'Monna Innominata' [first published in the *Pageant* vol., *Works,* pp. 58–64]. Such compound work has a connection (very often) which is of interest to the author and which <the reader> an editor gains nothing by discarding" (Penn. Hist. Soc. Gratz MSS, Case 11, Box 3). See above, Lttr. 133 and *Christina Rossetti,* pp. 28–29.

151 ❖ *Christina Rossetti to Alexander Macmillan*

30 Torrington Sq. W.C.
August 16. [1887] [1]

Dear Mr. Macmillan

Was it not by an oversight that postage and other carriage was omitted from my account yesterday? If so, please let me know how much I still owe, and I will send stamps.

Pray do not even in joke talk about my having "cut" you. I hope I am incapable of cutting any friend, and certainly I shall not pick out one who treats me kindly!

Very sincerely yours
Christina G. Rossetti

---

[1] Year date by firm.

152 ❖ *Christina Rossetti to Alexander Macmillan*

30 Torrington Square—W.C.
Monday morning. [August, 1887] [1]

Dear Mr. Macmillan

Mr. Gosse [2] answers:—

"There has been a blunder somewhere, probably at the publishing office of the 'Saturday Review' "—. He is now leaving for a 5 weeks' holiday, so I fear the matter cannot any longer be rectified: at any rate I do not see aught more for me to do.

I sent him your note of explanation without losing time; and his letter is the result, as I conclude.

I fancy it might be worth while for a "Pageant" to be sent to Rev^d. R. F. Littledale,[3] LLD.

9 Red Lion Square—W.C.,

as he is an influential person in more ways than one, and friendly towards [me]. I dare say you will kindly give the necessary order.

Very truly yours
Christina G. Rossetti

---

[1] Month and year date by firm.

[2] Sir Edmund Gosse. The only clue I can find to this obscure reference is an unfavorable review in *The Saturday Review* of WMR's *Life of Keats* (1887) which, as one of the *Great Writers* series, edited by Eric S. Robertson, was published that autumn. The book, wrote the *Saturday* reviewer, "ranks with the worst specimens of barren superfluity to be found in the series"; and William's criticism he stigmatized as "a continual affront, not only to the sensibility of the poetic, but likewise to common or human, intelligence" (Nov. 26, 1887), pp. 737–738. AM might have considered this verdict another evidence of what he called "Saturdayism," the mocking tone and occasional sneers of which, he once said, were "as intolerant as fire and faggot" (*Macm. Lttrs.,* Glasgow ed., pp. 66, 103, 246, *et passim*). In 1887 this journal, still owned by Beresford Hope, was edited by Walter Herries Pollock.

[3] Richard Frederick Littledale (1833–1890), a noted High Church theologian and controversialist, author of *Plain Reasons Against Joining the Church of Rome* (1880) and co-editor of the *Priests' Prayer Book* (1864). A friend highly valued by CGR, he was a good-humored Irishman with a penchant for writing witty verses to his friends.

153 ✧ *Christina Rossetti to Alexander Macmillan*

30 Torrington Square
W.C.
December 19. 1888.

Dear Mr. Macmillan

I have just received 4.4.0 from the Clarendon Press [1] for leave to reprint 4 pieces, so allow me to send you 2.2.0 as you and I

have a joint interest in the text. This, so far as I can recollect, is the first time such a matter has been in question between us.

But I suddenly wake up to the fact that I have heretofore
refused payment on more than one occasion. Was this, done
without your concurrence, fair towards your Firm? If unfair,
my worst error perhaps was when I arranged Goblin Market
for music and made an agreement that my friend alone should
set that particular piece, long since published by him.[2] What
shall I now do? If aggrieved by my vagaries, please set me a
lump sum and I will honour your bill.

May I, to so kind an old friend, express my delight at your
donation of a palace to our new London See?[3] I hear of you
and yours sometimes thro' my dear Henrietta Rintoul,[4] so I
have not quite lost sight of you.

I scarcely anticipate Christmas by now offering you my best
wishes.

Very sincerely yours
Christina G. Rossetti

---

[1] Macmillan was publisher for the Oxford University Press from 1863
to 1881, at which time the University assumed control of its own publications, conferring the degree of Honorary M.A. upon him in recognition of his services.

[2] Emanuel Aguilar (1824–1904) made a cantata of *Goblin Market*.

[3] CGR evidently misunderstood the circumstances. It was not a
"palace" that Macmillan donated, but his old home of Knapdale (The
Elms) at Tooting, which he had purchased in 1863 and for which he
retained a sentimental attachment because of its many happy associa-
tions. But since he had two other residences in 1888 (his country
establishment, Bramshott Chase, and a town house at 21 Portland Place),
and therefore no longer lived at Knapdale, he was obliged to dispose
of the property. Fearing that if he sold it, the house might fall into
unfriendly hands and be demolished, he preferred to present it to the
new Bishop of the Diocese of Rochester, who at the time had no available residence. Although the house was not occupied by succeeding
bishops, it remained Church property until 1905.

[4] See above, Lttr. 135 and n. 3.

5 Endsleigh Gardens.
N.W.
May 24th/89

Dear Mr. Macmillan,

Please excuse a very laconic presentment of the facts. Francis Hueffer,[1] Musical Critic of the Times, Author of the libretto of Colomba, of a volume on the Troubadours, of half a century of Music in England, etc. etc., died last Janr. aged 43 leaving a widow & three children[2] & little indeed in the way of property: a Memorial is being circulated asking that a Civil List Pension may be awarded to his widow. Would you be willing to sign the Memorial? or would you obtain other influential signatures, or put me in the way of obtaining them?

I should explain that Hueffer was a naturalized Englishman, an intimate friend of mine & his widow is the half sister of my wife.

The Memorial ought to be presented early in June.

Believe me
Very truly yours,
W. M. Rossetti

---

[1] Franz Hueffer (1846–1889), who Anglicized his name, was a German from a wealthy Roman Catholic family. Brilliant and learned, he came to England in 1868 and achieved distinction as a Wagnerian expert, musicologist and music critic, Schopenhauer scholar, and editor. In 1872 he married Catherine, Ford Madox Brown's younger daughter by his second wife, and thus became William's brother-in-law. His chief claim to fame today rests upon the fact that he was father to Ford Madox Hueffer (1873–1939), who in 1919 changed his name to Ford. See Richard M. Ludwig, "The Reputation of Ford Madox Ford," *PMLA* (Dec., 1961), pp. 544–552. See also Ford Madox Hueffer, *Ancient Lights* (1911), published in America as *Memories and Impressions*.

[2] They were Ford, Oliver, and Juliet. We may regard this letter, fitting conclusion to the series, as a lift from the old to the new literary generation. As usual in such cases, William was pursuing an immediate aim, all unaware of the fact that his efforts in behalf of the Hueffer family would achieve the larger end of smoothing the way for Ford Madox Ford, "the last of the Pre-Raphaelites," another writer of genius whose contributions have enriched our literature.

INDEX

❖◆❖

Academy, The, 105 and 106 n. 1, 109, 118 and n. 3, 140 n. 2

Aguilar, Emanuel, 157 and n. 2

Alexander, P. P., 68 n. 3

Allen, Grant, 108 n. 1, 134 n. 1

Allingham, William, 4, 18 and n. 2, 32 and n. 1, 45, 47, 76 n. 1

Alma-Tadema, Lawrence, 109 n. 1

Amor Mundi, 112 and n. 2

Angeli, Helen Rossetti, 66 n. 1

Annus Domini, 120 and 121 n. 3

Anson, Peter F., 101 n. 2

Apple Gathering, An, 59 and n. 3

Appleton, Charles, 118 n. 3

Argosy, 60 n. 1, 82 and 83 n. 1

Athenæum, The, 3, 33 n. 1, 45 and 46 n. 3, 53 n. 1, 89 n. 1, 100 n. 3, 105 and 106 n. 1, 118 n. 3, 140 n. 2

Austin, Mrs., 22 and n. 1

Baynes, R. H., 34 and n. 1, 35

Berry, Thomas, 8

Bevington, M. M., 68 n. 1

Birthday, A, 6, 59 and n. 3

Black, William, 98 and n. 3

Blackwood's, 102 and 103 n. 1

Blake, William, 14 and n. 3, 16 and 17 n. 2, 18 and nn. 1, 3, 21, 28 and nn. 1, 2, 68 n. 3

Blunt, John Henry, 25 and n. 2

Blunt, W. C., 25 n. 2

Boldemann, Mrs., 69

Borbould, E., 41 n. 3

Bowes, Robert, 15 n. 4

Boyd, Alice, 78 and n. 3, 79, 80, 81, 82, 83 n. 2, 85, 86–87 and 88 n. 1, 141 n. 2

Brett, George Edward, 136 n. 1

Brimley, Catherine, 95 and n. 2

Brown, Lucy Madox, 66 and n. 1, 98 n. 2, 120 and 121 n. 1

Brown, Oliver Madox, 117 n. 2

Browne, H. K., 41 n. 3

Browning, Robert, 18 and 19 n. 4

Burcham, Robert P., 124 n. 1

Bryant, William, 152, 153 and n. 1

Burn, James Frederick (James Robert), 38 and n. 2, 40, 42

Burne-Jones, Edward, 129 n. 3

Burroughs, John, 68 n. 2

Burrows, Henry William, 120 and 121 n. 3

Burton, William Shakespear, 151 n. 1

Burton, Mrs., 151 and n. 2

Butts, Captain, 18 and n. 1, 21

By the Waters of Babylon, 56 n. 2
Byron, Harriet Brownlow, 101 and
  n. 2

Caine, Hall, 140 n. 2
Called to be Saints, 120 and 121
  nn. 2, 4, 139 and 139 n. 2
Carlyle, John, 16 n. 2
Cary, Henry Francis, 16 n. 2
Cary's Academy, 62 n. 1
Cayley, Charles Bagot, 16 n. 2, 66
  and n. 1, 106 and 107 n. 3
Century, 99 n. 1, 108 n. 1
"Charlmont, Lucy," 84 n. 2
Christina Rossetti: poems in *Athenæum,* 3, 89 n. 1; in *Germ,* 3,
115 n. 2; writes *Goblin Market,*
5; photographs, 13 and nn. 1,
2; devotional pieces, 14; second
volume, 19, 23, 24 and n. 1; MS
notebooks, 22 and n. 2, 23; Macmillan's half-profits system, 23
and n. 1, 106, 107, 135 n. 1; in
Hastings, 33 and n. 1, 64 n. 1;
writes *Prince's Progress,* 33 n. 1,
46 and n. 3, 47, 49; reads proof,
37, 44, 45, 93, 94 n. 3, 112, 114,
137; attends Christ Church, 37
n. 1; second edition of *Goblin
Market,* 37, 39, 44, 45, 47; Dallas'
praise, 39 n. 3; visit to Italy, 47,
48 n. 1, 49, 51, 52 and 53 n. 2; to
Gloucester, 69 and 70 n. 2;
moves to Euston Square, 69 n.
3; to Torrington Square, 69 n.
3, 120 and 121 n. 1, 122 n. 1;
health, 70 n. 1, 93 and 94 n. 3,
95, 106, 123 and n. 2; complete
edition of works, 74, 79, 80, 84,
99, 105, 107, and illustrations
for, 113–114 and n. 1, 115; illustration of *Speaking Likenesses,* 100; at Eastbourne Hospital, 101 and n. 2, 103 and 104

nn. 2; Gemmer manuscript, 104
and 105 n. 1; unpublished
poems, 107 n. 1; visits Maria,
112 and 113 n. 1; devotional
prose, 120 and 121 nn. 2–4; business affairs, 126–128; thanks
Watts, 127 and 128 n. 3; copyright, 134 and n. 1, 135; at
Sevenoaks, 139 and n. 1; refuses
reprinting of poetry extracts,
154. See also *Goblin Market,
Prince's Progress, Speaking
Likenesses,* and titles of other
poems
Chronicle, The, 67 and 68 n. 2
Churchman's Shilling, 83 n. 1, 90
  and n. 1, 91 n. 2, 112 and n. 2
Clarendon Press, 156
Coleridge, Samuel Taylor, 5
Coleridge, Sir John, 134 n. 1
Colvin, Sidney, 89 n. 1
Commonplace, 78 and n. 4, 80, 81
  and n. 1, 82 and 83 n. 1, 85 and
  n. 1, 86 and n. 1, 88 and 89 n. 1
Comedy of Dante Allighieri, The,
  30–31 and n. 1
Comyn, Patrick, 68 n. 1
Consider, 56 n. 2
Cook, Keningale R., 70–71 and n.
  1
Copyright law, 134 and n. 1, 135
Cornhill Magazine, The, 4-5
Craig, Isa, 44 n. 1, 60 n. 1
Craik, George Lillie, 77 and 78 n.
  1, 139, 143
Crayon, 83 n. 1
Critic, The, 3
Cutts, H. W., 118 n. 5

Dallas, Eneas Sweetland, 39 n. 3
Dalziel Brothers, 54 n. 1, 93 and
  94 n. 1
Dante Gabriel Rossetti: painter

and poet, 3; artist friends, 4; seeks publication of his own and Christina's work, 4–6; MS of *Early Italian Poets* offered Macmillan, 4; shows Macmillan Christina's *Uphill,* 5; leases Tudor House, 16 and 17 n. 1; Cheyne Walk letterhead, 17 n. 1; subtenants, 17 n. 1; contributions to *Blake,* 16; edits Blake's unpublished poetry, 17 n. 2; Swinburne's friend, 2, 22, 25–30; *Venus Verticordia,* 30 and n. 2; in Paris, 32 n. 2; designs (*Inferno*), 37, 40 (*Prince's Progress*), 38 and n. 5, 49, 50, 51, 54, 61, 62; business details and *Prince's Progress,* 44 n. 1; proposes changes in Christina's poems, 47 n. 1, 55 n. 2; correction of signature, 49 and n. 1; woodcuts for *Tennyson,* 55 n. 1, 56; refuses to illustrate for Isa Craig, 60 n. 1; Ellis publishes *Poems,* 85 n. 1, 87, 88 n. 2; overdose of laudanum, 118 n. 6; recovers poems, 150 n. 2; posthumous exhibits, 150 and n. 2

Dante and His Circle. See *Early Italian Poets*

Davies, William, 127 and 128 n. 2

Dead Hope, 69 n. 1

Dennis, Imogene Rossetti, 22 n. 2

Dirge, A, 98 n. 2

Disraeli, Benjamin, 89 n. 1

Dobell, Bertram, 127 and 128 n. 1

Dodgson (Lewis Carroll), 63 n. 1

Dream Love, 44 n. 1

Dreamland, 115 n. 2

Early Italian Poets, 4

Echo, 34 and n. 2

Edinburgh Courant, 28, 67 and 68 n. 3

Eggleston, Edward, 108 n. 1

Eliot, George, 15 n. 3

Ellis, F. S., 74, 75, 76, 81–82, 85 n. 1

Ellis, Havelock, 103 n. 2

End, An, 115 n. 2

Endsleigh Gardens, 128 and 129 n. 1

Evans, Dr. Sebastian, 25 n. 2

Examiner, The, 109 and 110 n. 2, 118 n. 4

Faithfull, Emily, 44 and n. 1

Faulkner, Charles, 41 n. 2

Faulkner, Miss, 41 and n. 2

Fay, Gerda. See Gemmer, Caroline

Ferrier, James Frederick, 102 and 103 n. 1

Fine Art, chiefly Contemporary, 65 and n. 2, 66, 67 and 68 n. 1

Fine Arts Club, 150 and n. 2

Fleishman, S. L., 103 n. 2

Ford (Hueffer), Ford Madox, 158 n. 1

Ford, James A., 32, 33 n. 1, 43

Fraser, James, 15 n. 4

Fraser's Magazine, 15 n. 4, 18 n. 2, 67 and 68 n. 4

From House to Home, 34 and n. 1, 35 and n. 1, 39 n. 1

Froude, J. E., 68 n. 4

Gabriel, Miss, 34

Gaskell, Mrs., 6, 89 n. 1

Geikie, Alexander, 15 n. 4

Gemmer, Caroline, 45 and 46 and n. 2, 77 and n. 2, 80, 104 and 105 n. 1

Germ, The, 3, 115 and n. 2

Gilchrist, Alexander, 4, 14 n. 3. *See also* Blake, William

Gilchrist, Anne, 14 n. 3, 26 n. 2

Gilchrist, Herbert, 15 n. 3

Glasgow News, 117 n. 3

Goblin Market, 5, 6, 7, 13 n. 1, 19–20, 24, 31–32 and n. 1, 33 n. 1, 37, 38, 39, 40–41, 44 and n. 1, 45, 46, 47 and n. 1, 50, 63, 74, 76 and n. 1, 77 and n. 1, 80, 91, 98, 105, 154, 157 and n. 2
Golden Treasury series, 32 n. 1
Gosse, Sir Edmund, 7, 155 and 156 n. 2
Graphic, The, 90
Graves, C. L., 25 n. 2
Green, J. E., 2
Greenwell, Dora, 20 n. 2, 112 and 113 n. 1
Grove, George, 61 n. 1, 92 n. 4, 109, 110, 128 and 129 n. 2, 130 n. 1
Guardian, The, 47

Hake, George, 118 and n. 6
Hake, Thomas Gordon, 118 and n. 6
Hamber, Thomas, 118 n. 2
Hannay, James, 28 and n. 2, 68 n. 3
Hatton, Miss G. M., 107 n. 1
Heimann, Adolf H., 140 n. 4
Heimann, Amelia Barnard, 139 and 140 n. 4
Heine, Heinrich, 102 and 103 nn. 1, 2
Helen Grey, 56 n. 2
"Hero: a Metamorphosis," 60 n. 1, 82 and 83 n. 1
Holt, 102 and 103 n. 2
Holy Heavenly Chime, A, 144–145 and n. 1, 156 n. 2
Hope, Beresford, 27 n. 2, 156 n. 2
Hopkins, Ellice, 116
Hotten, 68 n. 1
Hour, The, 118 and n. 2, 118 and n. 6
Howell, Charles Augustus, 66 n. 1

Howell, Frances Catherine, 66 and n. 1
Hueffer, Francis (Franz), 118 n. 3, 158 and n. 1
Hughes, Arthur, 94 and n. 5, 96 and n. 2, 100, 102, 103 n. 2, 111 n. 1
Holman Hunt, 4

I Will Lift Up Mine Eyes to the Hills, 14 n. 1
If (*Hoping Against Hope*), 60 n. 1
Inferno (William Michael Rossetti's translation), 15, 16 n. 2, 33 n. 1, 37, 52, 53 n. 1, 95
Ingelow, Jean, 19, 20 n. 2, 39 n. 3, 58, 59 n. 2
Ingram, John H., 20 n. 1, 117 n. 2

James Clarke and Co., 147
James Parker & Co., 121 n. 3
Jenner, Sir William, 70 n. 1, 101 n. 2

Keary, Annie, 98 and n. 3
Keene, C., 41 n. 3
Kingsley, Charles, 1
Knapdale, 70 n. 2, 157 and n. 3
Knight, Joseph, 90 and 91 n. 3

Lancashire cotton hands, 60 n. 1. *See also* Craig, Isa
Last Night, 45 and 46 n. 1
Leifchild, Henry and Franklin, 106 and 107 n. 3
Leland, F. R., 150 n. 2
Life of Keats, 156 n. 2
Linton, William James, 54 n. 1, 61, 62, 63
Little, Brown & Co. *See* Roberts Brothers
Littledale, Richard Frederick, 156 n. 3

London Review, 7, 62, 67 and 68 n. 1
Longfellow, Henry Wadsworth, 16 n. 2
"Lost Titian, The," 83 n. 1
Lothrop, Daniel, 147 and n. 1
Lowest Room, The, 20 n. 2, 23 n. 1
Lyra Eucharistica, 14 n. 1

McClennan, John Ferguson, 1
McColl, Norman, 89 n. 1
MacLehose, James, 28 n. 1
Mackail, J. W., 92 n. 3
Mackay, Charles, 68 n. 1
Macmillan, Alexander: meets William Rossetti, 1; to London, 2; *Macmillan's Magazine,* 3, 23 n. 1; "Tobacco Parliaments," 4; sees Christina Rossetti's poems, 5; business acumen, 7–8; move to London, 15 n. 4; publisher to Oxford University, 15 n. 4, 157 n. 1; letters about Swinburne, 21, 25–26 and nn. 1, 2; system of half profits, 23 and 24 n. 1, 106, 107, 135 n. 1; death of son, 64 n. 1; Upper Tooting, 70 n. 2; death of wife, 95 and n. 2; second marriage, 106 and 107 n. 2; to Italy, 106 and 107 n. 2, 108; protests piracy, 108 n. 1; appreciation of Christina, 116; business arrangement with Christina, 126–127; on copyright, 134 n. 1, 135 and n. 1; degree from Oxford, 157 n. 1; residences, 157 n. 3; gives Knapdale to church, 157 n. 3
Macmillan, Daniel, 1, 2
Macmillan, Frederick, 113 n. 2, 136 n. 1
Macmillan, George, 70 n. 2, 113 and n. 2, 114

Macmillan Brothers, 1, 2, **4, 15 n.** 4, 16 n. 3, 136 and n. 1
Macmillan's Bibliographical Catalogue, 30 and 31 n. 1, 102 and 103 n. 1
Macmillan's Magazine, 6, 23 and n. 1, 45 and 46 n. 1, 56 n. 2, 59 and n. 3, 69 n. 1, 98 nn. 2, 3, 103 and 104 n. 1, 108 n. 1, 109, 110, 116, 128 and 129 n. 3, 131, 148 and n. 1
Magnússon, 92 n. 3
Maiden Song, 15 n. 3
Marillier, H. C., 30 n. 2
Marston, Philip Bourke, 89 n. 1
Masson, David, 3, 6, 8, 23 n. 1, 44, 45, 56, 60
Maude Clare, 59 and n. 3
Maurice, J. F. D., 1
Meredith, George, 17 n. 1
Millais, John Everett, 41 n. 3
Minto, William, 110 n. 2, 118 n. 4
Monna Innominata, 154 n. 3
Morgan, Charles, 1, 6, 8, 16 n. 3, 28 n. 1, 38 n. 2
Morley, John, 98 n. 3
Morning Star, The, 45
Morris, William, 66, 92 nn. 2, 3, 129 n. 3, 130
Mortara, Cavalier, 25 n. 1
Mortara, Conte, 25 and n. 1, 27
Mother Country, 69 and n. 1
Mott, Frank Luther, 146 n. 1
Moxon, Edward, 54 n. 1
My Friend, 23 n. 1
Munro, Alexander, 4, 17 and n. 3
Murray, Charles Fairfax, 60 n. 1, 75 n. 1, 78, 79, 111 n. 1, 138 and 139 n. 3

Niles, Thomas, 58, 59 n. 2, 66, 93
Nonconformist, The, 52
Norton, Caroline, 7

"Nowhere." See *Speaking Likenesses*

Nursery Rhymes (Sing-Song), 74 and n. 2, 75, 76, 77–78, 79, 84

O Roses for the Flush of Youth, 115 n. 2

Offering of the New Law, The, 14 n. 1

Old and New Years Ditties, 154 n. 3

Olivieri, Agostino, 148–149 and n. 1, 150 and n. 1

Once a Week, (periodical) 59 n. 3

One Day, 20

Oxford and Cambridge Magazine, 3

Pageant and Other Poems, A, 133 and nn. 1, 2, 137 and n. 1

Palgrave, F. T., 7, 66 and n. 1, 68 n. 5

Pall Mall Gazette, 88 n. 2, 89 n. 1

Passing Away, 63 and 64 n. 1, 154 n. 3

Patton, Sir Noel, 143 n. 1

Pause of Thought, A, 115 n. 2

Penkill Castle, 78 n. 3, 141 n. 2

Pictorial World, 118 and n. 5

Pignatel, Emma, 106 and 107 n. 2, 108

Piracy by American publishers, 108 n. 1

Polidori, Charlotte and Eliza, 115 n. 1,, 121 n. 1

Polidori, Gaetano, 3

Polydore, Henry, 69 and 70 n. 2

Pollock, Walter Herries, 156 n. 2

Pratt, Ella Farman, 146 and n. 1, 147

Pre-Raphaelite Brotherhood, 66 n. 1

Prince's Progress, 33 n. 1, 38 and n. 5, 42 and n. 1, 45 and 46 n. 3, 47, 48 n. 1, 49, 50–51, 54 and n. 1, 55, 56, 60, 61, 63, 119, 122, 127

Proctor, Adelaide, 19 and 20 n. 1

"Pros and Cons," 82 n. 1

Prose stories. See *Commonplace*

Putt, Gorley, 153 n. 1

Quilter, Harry, 128 and 129 n. 3, 130 n. 2, 131, 132

Repining, 115 n. 2

Rintoul, Henrietta, 139 and 140 n. 3, 157 and n. 4

Rivington, J. A., 63 and n. 1, 64 n. 1

Roberts, Lewis A., 59 n. 3

Roberts Brothers, 58–59 and n. 2, 83 n. 1, 93, 108, 136, 137

Robertson, Eric S., 156 n. 2

Rossetti family, 2–3, 37 n. 1, 69 n. 3. *See also* Christina, Dante Gabriel, William

Rossetti, Frances Lavinia, 3, 16 n. 2, 53 and nn. 2, 5, 121 n. 1

Rossetti, Gabriel Arthur, 144 and 145 n. 2

Rossetti, Gabriele, 3, 140 n. 4

Rossetti, Helen Maria, 144 and 145 n. 2. *See also* Angeli

Rossetti, Maria Francesca, 3, 37 n. 2, 69 n. 3, 101 n. 2, 127 and 128 n. 1

Rossetti, Mary Elizabeth Madox and Michael Ford Madox, 135 and n. 2

Rossetti, Olivia Frances Madox, 144 and 145 n. 1

Round Tower at Jhansi, 59 and n. 3

Routledge Brothers, 90, 96 n. 2, 111 and n. 1

Royal Academy, 150 and n. 2
Royal Princess, A, 44 n. 1
Ruskin, John, 4, 5

"Safe Investment, A," 83 n. 1
Sandys, Frederick, 112 n. 2
Saturday Review, The, 7, 27 and
   n. 2, 68 n. 1, 155 and 156 n. 2
Schlesinger, 111 and n. 2
Scott, William Bell, 55 n. 1, 66, 68
   n. 3, 78 n. 3, 88 n. 1, 109 and 110
   n. 1, 116
Seasons, 56 n. 2
Secularist, The, 117 n. 3
Sedgewick, Arthur G., 108 n. 1
Seek and Find, 138 and 139 n. 3
Seeley's bookshop, 2
Sharp, William (Fiona McLeod),
   143 and n. 1, 144 and 145 n. 1
Shilling Magazine. See *Church-
   man's Shilling*
Shipley, Orby, 14 and n. 1
Shorthouse, J. Henry, 135 n. 1
Sing-Song, 74, 75, 76, 77, 80, 89,
   90, 92, 93 and n. 1, 94 and nn.
   3, 5, 96 and n. 2, 100, 111 and n.
   1. See also *Nursery Rhymes*
Sister Maude, 114–115 and n. 1
Sleep at Sea, 39 n. 1
Smetham, James, 62 and n. 1, 100
Smile and a Sigh, A, 69 n. 1
Smith, Miss, 35 n. 1
Smith and Elder, 4, 32, 33 n. 1
SPCK (Society for Propagation of
   Christian Knowledge), 121 n.
   2, 138 and 139 nn. 2, 3
Solomon, Simeon, 93 and 94 n. 4
Songs in a Cornfield, 54 and 55 n.
   2
Speaking Likenesses, 98 and n. 1,
   100 and n. 1, 101, 103 and 104
   nn. 1, 2, 105, 106 n. 1
Spectator, The, 3
Spring Fancies, 45 and 46 n. 1

Stephens, F. G., 66 and n. 1
Stern, Madeleine B., 59 n. 2
Stillman, William, 81, 83 n. 1
Stuart, Dorothy, 34 n. 2
Sudden Light, 61 n. 1
Sunday Times, The, 90 and 91 n.
   3
Sweet Death, 115 n. 2
Swinburne, Algernon Charles, 17
   n. 1, 18 and n. 3, 21–22, 25–30,
   26 nn. 1, 2, 30 n. 1, 31, 38 and n.
   5, 83 n. 1, 129 n. 3, 130 and n. 3

Tadema. *See* Alma-Tadema
Taylor, Tom, 41 and n. 3, 47
Tebbs, Henry Virtue, 150 n. 2
Tenniel, R. A. J., 41 n. 3
Tennyson, Lord Alfred, 7, 22, 54
   n. 1, 69, 70 n. 1
Testimony, A, 115 n. 2
Thackeray, William Makepeace,
   4, 28 n. 2
Thomson, James, 117 n. 3
Times, The, 38, 39 and n. 3
Tissot, J., 41 and n. 3, 43
"Tobacco Parliaments," 4, 17 n. 3

Universal Review, 130 n. 2
University Magazine, The [Dub-
   lin], 71 n. 1
Uphill, 5, 6, 59 and n. 3

"Vanna's Twins," 83 n. 1
Venus Verticordia, 30 and n. 2

Watts-Dunton, Walter Theodore,
   118 n. 4, 126–128 n. 3, 130 n. 3,
   140 n. 2
"Waves of this Troublesome
   World," 83 n. 1
Westminster Review, 67, 68 n. 5
Whistler, James McNeill, 130 n. 2
Whitman, Walt, 15 n. 3, 68 n. 2
Who Shall Deliver Me?, 60 n. 1

Wideawake, 144 and 145 n. 1, 146 and n. 1, 147

William Michael Rossetti: meets Macmillan, 1, 2; at Cambridge, 3; at Excise Office, 3, art critic, 3, 27 and n. 2, 68 nn. 1, 4; translates Dante's *Inferno,* 15; 19 cantos of *Purgatorio,* 52 n. 1; criticizes *Blake,* 17–18; annotates catalogue of Blake's paintings, 17 n. 2; publishes (*Inferno*), 16 nn. 1, 2, 30 and 31 n. 1, 32 and 33 n. 1 (poetry), 53 (*Fine Art*), 65 and n. 2, 124, 132 n. 1; reviews Swinburne's *Poems,* 67 and 68 n. 1; marriage, 66 n. 1, 120 n. 1; at Euston Square, 69 n. 3, 120 n. 1; Macmillan and *Goblin Market,* 74, 76 and n. 1, 77 and n. 1; reviews Scott's *Poems,* 109 and 110 n. 1, 116; gout, 125 and n. 2; writes *Life of Keats,* 155 and 156 n. 2

Willis and Sotheran, 52

Wilson, John ("Christopher North"), 102 and 103 n. 1

Wintry Sonnet, A, 148 and n. 1

Wood, Mrs. Henry, 60 n. 1

Woods, Miss M. A., 154 and n. 2

Woolner, Thomas, 4, 66 and n. 1

Wordsworth, William, 134 n. 1

"Young Plants and Polished Corners," 120 and 121 n. 4. See also *Called to be Saints*